FOR CEO'S TRANSFORMING 2ND TIER FINANCIAL SERVICES ORGANISATIONS

BUILDING THE FOUNDATIONS FOR FUTURE SUSTAINABILITY M+A'S EXPANSION AND GROWTH

The CEO Secret Advantage

8 IMMEDIATE RE-SET STRATEGIES ADDRESSING THE MOST COMMON FAILINGS OF LEADERSHIP THROUGH TRANSFORMATIONAL CHANGE

Dr Miranda Jensen

Australia's Leading Specialist on 'Real-Time Transformations' for CEO's who need faster, more effective delivery of their Vision

First Published by Busybird Publishing, Melbourne, Australia, 2019

© 2019 Miranda Jensen

ISBN
Print: 978-0-6484789-6-6
Ebook: 978-0-6484789-7-3

All rights reserved. No part of this publication may be reproduced, distributed, or transmitted in any form or by any means, including photocopying, recording, or other electronic or mechanical methods, without the prior written permission of the publisher, except in the case of brief quotations embodied in critical reviews and certain other non-commercial uses permitted by copyright law.

First Edition

Credits
Editor: Kristen Corrects
Layout and typesetting: Busybird Publishing

Busybird Publishing
2/118 Para Road
Montmorency, Victoria
Australia 3094
www.busybird.com.au

Testimonials

'We can all choose to change and take the lead, or be forced to change – either way, change is almost something of a constant for organisations today. In her latest offering, Dr Jensen clearly outlines the need for change, and the need for a change in how organisation's address change to achieve successful transformation.

'Dr Jensen addresses the necessary tools of change, and more importantly addresses the thinking senior leaders need to understand to lead effective transformation; she presents these concepts in a structured yet flexible, easy-to-understand and pragmatic approach.

'What sets Dr Jensen's thinking apart is her focus on "embedding an ongoing, dynamic, real-time approach", which should help ensure the changes you initiate become the transformations you want and need. True to her own advice that "the key mantra for any external resources to internal resources should be *How can I make YOU successful?* With this book Dr Jensen provides tools, thinking and approaches to help make YOU successful."

Simon Higgins
Principal
Gently Consulting

'Change is scary for many people and organisational change even more so, as it disrupts and destabilises a huge part of our lives. It disheartens me to say that I've seen organisational change managed badly on many occasions, particularly in the financial services sector. I was beyond excited when I experienced Dr Miranda Jensen's Transformation³ model. It is, quite simply, the best and most pragmatic model I have encountered. Even more importantly – it works! If you want true transformation then look no further. This is it.'

Teresa Hetherington
Director
Corporate Wisdom (Australia) Pty Ltd

'In the last 15 years, 52% of the Fortune 500 companies have disappeared. Not only do companies need to ensure they have a 10 year+ Future Strategy in place, they need the practical skills to transform their organisation. The incremental approaches to change are no longer relevant in the hyper-accelerating world we now operate in.

'In this book you will find an approach that is both easy to apply, whilst also opening you to a new way of thinking about change. Miranda's phenomenological research led her to a powerful model in understanding how we transform - the value of which, can take a lifetime to achieve. It is an invaluable contribution for us all.'

David Harris
CEO
Futures Strategy

'Transformational cultural change within financial services is one of the most significant challenges facing the industry today. Such change is not easy, needing focus and drive, along with considerable effort from all involved to be successful. This book provides a practical framework, tools, thinking and ideas to support smaller organisations work their way successfully through transformational change, without the need of an army of external resources. Having used this approach myself to guide the delivery of change, I highly recommend this book as a simple, practical and insightful handbook for the transformation we all face.'

Sally Stares
General Manager, People and Change
Catholic Church Insurance Limited

*'If you are depressed you are living in the past.
If you are anxious you are living in the future.
If you are at peace you are living in the present.'*

Lao Tzu

Contents

Foreword	i
Preface	iii
Introduction	xi

Section 1 – How Things Transform — 1

1. The Landscape Has Changed	3
2. The Theory That Fails	7
3. The Art of How Things Transform	13
4. Big Change Ahead	21
5. Transformation^3 – The Elements	25

Section 2 – Organisations in Transition — 35

6. The Role of Culture ...	37
7. Application of Transformation^3	45
8. Understanding the Activities to Undertake	49
9. Balancing the Elements	101

Section 3 – Skills for a Secret Advantage — 113

10. Creating a Space — 115
11. Framing in Change and Transformation — 125
12. Successful Change Builds Confidence — 131
13. The Change Armour — 135
14. Responses to Change — 147
15. When the Ground Beneath You Shifts — 153
16. Empowerment — 163
17. Change in Leadership — 167
18. Getting it Right — 175
19. We've Got This — 183
20. Core Capabilities — 187
21. Transformation^3 for Personal Growth — 193
22. A New Way of Thinking — 197

Epilogue — 201

Foreword

The recent Royal Commission into Financial Services, and the guiding principles (and soon to be legislative changes) that stem from it highlight once and for all the significance of the focus on customers and doing the right things the right way as essential components of the license to operate a services business.

One could say with increasing comfort that focus on customers and behaviours even usurps the importance of returns to shareholders and the significance of embedding technological developments, or at least that customer and behaviour focus are 'the right to play'.

Smaller organisations, particularly those operating under mutual or customer–owned principles are in a unique position to embed customer and behaviour focus more swiftly than larger organisations and indeed use such developments as a new 'first-mover-advantage', particularly in a space where people are actively looking for evidence of organisations acting in customer interest as a precursor to dealing with them.

Whilst perhaps a generalisation, the willingness of people who have chosen to work for a customer-owned / mutual organisation will more easily understand the importance of behaving in customers' interests when compared to employees of organisations that have listened to the constant espousing of shareholder interests and profits. Simply put, cultural transformation focused on doing what's right should be easier in smaller places.

CEOs of smaller organisations should therefore now be energised by the opportunity to embark on cultural and behavioural transformation, centred on doing the right thing, the right way by customers. This is not of course to the exclusion of continuing to embed essential tech and data orientated service model change.

However, the fact that good customer-centric behaviour is far more difficult to replicate than technology means that the focus on cultural transformation should in this day and age actually lead developments in operating models.

Roberto Scenna
Chief Executive Officer
Catholic Church Insurance Limited

Preface

The question that I am most asked is: 'How did you become a specialist in transforming organisations?' This line of questioning usually includes 'what did you study?' and when I provide an overview of my PhD thesis am met with 'how fascinating/amazing/interesting/intriguing'. So by way of preface for this book and to provide early enlightenment on what 'secrets' will be divulged in these pages, I will respond to this typical line of enquiry accordingly!

My background is as a performing artist. I studied opera as my undergraduate at the Victorian College of the Arts. Through my formative years I was drawn to the arts for their sense of connectedness to the human experience, the emotional understandings, storytelling and passion that they explore. However, whilst I enjoyed the technical proficiency of opera, I came to find that the relevance of stories were failing to connect with new audiences. As such, after completing my honors year, I pressed pause on performing classical works to explore contemporary music. I released 4 contemporary solo albums exploring new technologies in sound production and storytelling with modern relevance.

In parallel, I found that all the many skills developed as an artist were transferable into the corporate world and soon found myself highly engaged in organisational transformations. There were two factors that led to a shift in focus from 'artist' to transformation specialist. Firstly, I found that facilitating individuals and organisations through change provided a level of 'two-way' interaction that was never going to exist in a 'performer/audience' relationship. Secondly, the early transformation projects I was involved in had such significance in people's lives that it was abundantly clear that the social contribution we can make through being a change innovator/leader/adopter/influencer creates ripple waves in the community for future generations, that to me, was unparalleled in how I could contribute purely in the arts.

These early transformation programs included Regionalising the Department of Justice, Cultural Change at Consumer Affairs Victoria, the establishment of the Victorian Commission for Gambling and Liquor Regulation and the Independent Broad-based Anti-corruption Commission.

In this journey of leveraging unique skills and identifying 'how and where to deliver my highest value', I was struck by the words of Justine Musk:

'Move between worlds, speak both languages, connect the tribes, mash the elements to spark fresh creative insight until you wake up with the epiphany that changes your life.'

This epiphany occurred for me whilst undertaking my PhD where I wanted to explore: What are the greatest learnings I can take from music to enhance how we change and transform in organisations and as individuals?

Whilst it wasn't clear to me at the outset, through the research, I developed a deep understanding of how things transform. I landed a real-time model for assessing and responding to the needs of organisations and individuals as they are transforming.

I am fortunate to have had a thesis topic that I found thoroughly engaging, relevant and meaningful. Corporate peers have highlighted that the findings of the research are something that can 'take a lifetime to realise'. The topic was 'A Phenomenological Enquiry into Pythagorean Tuning in the Creation of New Music.' If this title has you somewhat confused I shall, as I have each time I've responded to this question, break it down:

Phenomenology essentially explores 'what is the human experience of ...'

Pythagorean Tuning is an early musical scale built on the pure 3/2 ratio. Named after its creator the ancient Greek philosopher, Pythagoras. The frequencies in this scale arguably have a richer resonance.

In the thesis title: 'creation of new music' could almost equally be replaced with 'creation of new experiences' as I had a startling revelation partway through the research where (in Justine Musk's words) my two 'worlds' sparked fresh creative insights!

I had tuned my acoustic piano to the Pythagorean frequencies and had been observing the human experience of practicing, song writing and improvising with the Pythagorean Tuning. I realised that the frequencies (with their richer resonance) became a benchmark for how I wanted to feel. Whilst at the same time they showed me how I was feeling (i.e. whether I was in alignment with the resonance), lastly I realised that the music I would play (whether it be one repeated note, a song or improvised) would help shift me from where I was to where I wanted to be.

I quickly 'white-boarded' these three elements: where I was, where I wanted to be, and what was helping to shift me and overlaid this thinking with best practice change management methodology. Through extensive analysis, testing and further developing this initial observation I landed a real-time way of ensuring effective transformations.

This real-time understanding of 'how things transform' has underpinned all my corporate engagements over the last 4 years with a number of professional licensees now trained in the Transformation[3] approach. It is a particularly powerful model as it is straightforward on the surface, familiar and easily applied. However, as the transforming environments become more complex, the model provides countless ways of identifying and addressing the many, varied challenges we face in organisational transformations.

With the Royal Commission into Misconduct in the Banking, Superannuation and Financial Services Industry (Royal Commission) final report released in February 2019 there are additional pressures for Financial Services (FS) leaders. Regardless of whether a Financial Services organisation needs to address its existing practices, is at risk of identifying misconduct in its organisation or is monitoring industry changes for impacts to its own operations the spotlight is firmly on this industry at this time. The increased scrutiny, expectations from consumers and revised regulatory environment all culminate in a destabilised operating environment.

In corporate organisations five years ago there was still discussion on whether an organisation was just implementing incremental changes (a system upgrade or a re-org, etc.) or whether they were fundamentally transforming who they are, and as a result implementing a transformation program. Often, the first step in supporting an organisation to transform was, in fact, assisting the organisation to understand that as they were holistically reviewing their operating model, structure, products and services, identity, technology and culture, they were undertaking a transformation program.

Fast-forward to now and my view is that all organisations are constantly transforming and need to develop the awareness and skills to adapt to the continued and exacerbated pace of change. The external pressures identified through environmental scanning practices can no longer be considered as isolated likelihoods to be addressed.

Consider for example, the downstream impacts of innovation and change in the automotive industry. Electric and driver-less vehicles will likely impact, significantly, on manufacturing and servicing practices, retailers including petrol stations and resources such as coal and oil. As these incremental changes occur the industry, and our lives will be transformed.

The incremental changes that are occurring in FS are similarly prompting organisational transformations. The Royal Commission, in particular, is fundamentally addressing the culture of our financial institutions. In doing so, it has raised the profile, perceptions and expectations consumers have on their service providers.

Specifically, it is Recommendation 5.6 (changing culture and governance) from the FS Royal Commission final report that will trigger the most significant and lasting change in the financial services landscape.

The recommendation specifies:

All financial services entities should, as often as reasonably possible, take proper steps to:

- *assess the entity's culture and its governance;*
- *identify any problems with that culture and governance;*
- *deal with those problems; and*
- *determine whether the changes it has made have been effective.*

In my view this recommendation very clearly says 'All FS entities – Transform your Organisation'. Or in the words of treasurer, Josh Frydenberg, 'the sector must change, and change forever'.

Following the release of the report, media, attention and commentary has been placed largely on Tier 1, top 4 practices and their response to the final report submission. Specific groups within the sector with direct impacts have also been on the front foot to respond and put plans into action. These immediate responses, whilst visible, will only play a small role in what will be a fundamental overhaul of the financial services industry – this will occur when the amount of change occurring in each individual organisation reaches a tipping point and we look back as a society and say 'remember when' or 'how did we operate like that'.

2nd tier FS providers are in a unique position with a change paradigm of 'lead or be led'. Meaning, many smaller, non-profit or community-focused operations have less concerns regarding their consumer identity (they are leading the way on what it means to be customer – or member – driven). However, these organisations are challenged to keep up with the pace of change in technology and services, (they are being led by innovation advancements occurring in Tier 1 companies).

For leaders in Financial Services organisations at present the key challenge is: How do I ensure my organisation is ethically undertaking its activities? How do I ensure our culture is one that identifies and calls out inappropriate behaviours? How do we unearth systemic processes and practices that leave us exposed? How do we stay abreast of emerging trends and establish or maintain our position as an industry leader?

What can be uncomfortable to consider is 'what your response would be' if you uncovered or contributed to unethical corporate practice. It is very easy following an investigation and with hindsight to say 'they should have' or 'I would have' but in so many instances it is the corporate culture (the way we do things around here) that normalises unacceptable attitudes, behaviours and practices.

This book aims to provide a thorough understanding of how to effectively transform your organisation. Including the fundamental culture that underpins everything that you do. The insights provided are intended to not only meet the pressure to remain competitive and ensure the organisations sustainability but to deeply consider where you are, where you want to be and just how it is that you will get there.

Introduction

The process of managing change is a requirement of the modern organisation. It comprises of a range of approaches that are utilised to assist with the human responses that individuals have in times of change. Organisations invest heavily in managing their staff through this process. The success of whether people adopt the changes can substantially affect the bottom line and has a lasting impact on culture and engagement. Organisations need to continually change to ensure a sustainable future in the fast-paced world of today.

For Financial Services organisations the recent Royal Commission has rightly focused on 'Why' instances of misconduct have occurred and what needs to change to ensure that these systemic industry issues are addressed, the 'What Now?' The fundamentals of change management are based on these two questions, having a clear understanding of 'what's not working' (the why) and having a clear shared vision of what needs to change (the what). With this in mind the Royal Commission, particularly its focus on these two themes, has been a powerful trigger for significant change in the Financial Services Industry.

WHY THIS BOOK IS REQUIRED

Since the 1980s, the focus in the change management practice has been on managing incremental changes in organisations; using a new system, a new structure or a new service offering as examples. In the last decade, the global pace of change has resulted in organisations undertaking all of these at once. The concept of transforming an organisation rather than just implementing changes has resulted from this quickening across the globe. Until recently, transformations have been managed using the same 'change management practices' as though they were individual incremental changes but on a larger scale.

The global quickening is accelerating due to disruptive technologies providing new experiences, ideas and expectations at a faster rate than ever before. Organisations are being driven to change from all angles: industry, technology, people, stakeholders and markets at an unprecedented rate and in more complex environments.

An organisations resources (both people and financial), are being consumed by the effort invested in incremental changes that are often obsolete by the time they are implemented. Organisations that are keeping pace seem to have the gift of foresight, as visionaries invest heavily in exploring and understanding the future. This is not always practicable and not every organisation can afford to keep at the current pace let alone predict and plan for the future. In the current de-stabilised Financial Services Industry this is more so a concern as some organisations are waiting to 'follow the leaders' and others are innovating and leading the way. The question of revolutionary or evolutionary change is being considered by Financial Services executive teams trying to predict industry responses and trends over the next 3-5 years.

To meet these demands a more dynamic approach to understanding and responding to transforming organisations in real time is required.

HOW THIS BOOK WILL HELP

This offering builds on the skills and experience that executive leaders have acquired in implementing programs with traditional change management practices.

It identifies the challenges often experienced in traditional change practices, such as the common scenario of being reactive and trying to gain buy-in and staff involvement at the implementation point of a program. This can easily be addressed by bringing change activities to the front of the program, minimising risk, testing approaches, and seeking early adopters, early.

The approach detailed throughout this book provides a way to unearth and resolve problems before they impact the success of a program – based on a tried and tested model of 'balancing the elements'.

This book introduces a new way of thinking about individuals and organisations in transition. It is the consideration of *'how things transform'* and explores not only what is being experienced but 'why' it is being experienced. This provides for practical and immediate ways to 'shift' the experience of impacted individuals through the change journey with positive and beneficial outcomes.

This new way of thinking, the practice of 'balancing the elements' can be seen and experienced in all facets of an individual's and organisation's experiences. It will continue to grow and evolve the more the elements are observed and reflected upon. The methodology comprises of 3 core elements and is called Transformation[3].

Transformation[3] builds upon the traditional approaches to change management that provide the tools and templates, steps and know-how for the strategic and transactional activities to manage change. The Transformation[3] approach provides a framework for the skills required to manage large scale complex change, in real time. Many organisations have implemented standardised change frameworks that contain a suite of documents to manage change, only to realise that they are missing the skilled individuals who can identify the needs of the organisation whilst it is transforming. This book introduces the Transformation[3] approach so that CEOs and their executive teams in the Financial Services Industry can be prepared for the transformation of their organisations over the next 3-5 years as a result of increased community expectations regulatory changes and increased competitiveness.

The Transformation[3] approach provides for a shared language and way of understanding what is being experienced by individuals and organisations in transition. As an executive team become familiar with observing 'how their organisation is (or isn't) transforming', the capabilities can be built throughout all levels, creating a change capable organisation that self-manages in sync with the new pace of change.

WHO THIS BOOK IS FOR

This book has been written to address the needs of CEOs and executive teams in the Financial Services Industry implementing transformational change in their organisation. This book makes the framework accessible for anyone who plays a role in implementing change: the change leaders. It acknowledges the diverse audience groups that come together to make change happen. It assists change leaders to be aligned in their thinking and consider ways of managing the organisation in transition.

The book is equally valuable for those who are part of an implementation. This could include individuals wishing to develop their leadership skills, particularly with a focus on managing change. It is also valuable for project team members and individuals wishing to build a better understanding of how organisations transform. In fact, the more people involved in understanding the model, the greater the ability to self-manage through periods of change and to support peers in an organisation in transition.

Whilst the book has been written for senior executives, it is important to note that we are all leaders in our own way. There may be skills, activities and techniques outlined that would apply more to those leading change rather than those experiencing change, but they are useful to understand. We model behaviours by supporting the changes being implemented, and we drive innovation by getting involved, contributing and by helping to shape the change and by encouraging others to do so also. In this way, this book will be beneficial across all areas and levels of an organisation to understand why a transformation is being managed in the way that it is and provide a guide for how everyone can contribute to its success. It would be appropriate and highly beneficial for an executive implementing against the Transformation[3] approach to provide the book, materials or excerpts to staff throughout the transition to be 'open and transparent' around how the change is being managed and why.

The term 'organisation' is used broadly and can be defined as '*an organised group of people with a particular purpose, such as a business or government department or a research organisation.*' The application of Transformation[3] can be equally applied in communities, schools, institutions, hospitals, small businesses, community clubs and associations. Whilst the activities in each element may differ in name, nature and size the basic premise of the model applies.

On an individual level, the model can be applied to personal experiences and life transformations. Chapter 21 introduces how the approach can be applied to individuals and is a beneficial tool for coaching and mentoring whether within a professional or personal development context.

It can be helpful whilst learning the concepts of 'balancing the elements' to apply the thinking to community or personal examples. This brings the model to life in new ways and deepens our understanding of how things transform in a general sense, which enables us to see more deeply, how your organisation can effectively transform.

WHAT IS INCLUDED IN THE BOOK

The book provides a brief history on change management and how to succeed, where traditional practices have often failed. The book introduces the Transformation³ methodology and concept for balancing the elements. The book explains the types of activities that would be completed during an organisational transformation including some detail on what they are, when to undertake the activity, why it is important, and what happens if it is missing. This detailed content can be seen as 'optional' content or as a reference section once your transformation is underway.

Many of the activities in the Transformation³ model are standard organisational activities, so this book does not provide a 'how-to' guide for each. However, the text does provide a summary on how each of the activities are beneficial during a transformation. This is the understanding that completing activities purely because they are contained in a project schedule can leave them being ineffective. Ensuring activities realise their benefits requires the right focus, drivers, inclusiveness, and timing to ensure their individual success and enable the transformation to occur.

The Transformation³ model is built on '*Must Haves*' and '*Nice to Haves*' to ensure an organisations transformation success. The model is flexible and scalable to the nature of the change being implemented. There are some concepts that will be restated throughout the book with the aim of 'embedding' this thinking so that it becomes a new way of viewing your organisation as it is transforming.

The book also provides simple techniques and refreshers including reframing, language, and ways of ensuring success. The book details the humanistic elements of leading and responding to change, providing frameworks for the behaviours experienced at certain points in a transition and the core change leadership skills that will assist those leading and supporting change to be successful.

What is not included is training on traditional change management practices or how to undertake particular activities traditionally associated with change. The book is focused on how things transform and should be viewed as additional knowledge and ways of thinking for managing complex transformations rather than a 'how-to' guide for managing change.

For the purposes of this book, individuals of any position who are facilitating change in their workplace will hereafter be called 'change leaders'. This may include CEOs, executives, directors, project directors, change managers or change consultants, change agents and impacted staff.

Section 1
How Things Transform

1

The Landscape Has Changed

In the last 50 years we've seen so much change in the world and at a quickening pace. Television. Computers. The internet. Mobile Phones. Social Media. In parallel there has been the emergence and development of change management as a practice. In the 1960s a sociologist was inspired by the adoption of new agricultural technologies. At this time, there was a quickening of innovation in the agricultural field and a drive in the industry to improve on traditional practices. From this, the concept of the '*Diffusion of Innovations*' was born. This theory has translated directly into modern change management practices with the categorisation of Innovators, Early Adopters, Early Majority, Late Majority and Laggards. The focus in these early models was on communication channels and started to explore themes of critical mass and the tipping point.

The Management Consulting era in the 1980s saw the change management industry being born in earnest. As the technological innovations have quickened since this time, so has the speed of change and the need for efficient and effective adoption. It was around this time that superannuation and investment products increased, leading to an increased role for financial advisors which, in turn, changed the landscape of the Financial Services Industry.

The idea of the '*burning platform*' was introduced and inspired new methodologies and change practices throughout the 1990s.

The rate of change in the 2000s, for many, felt insurmountable, with many leaders becoming frustrated with top-down failures. There was more widespread use of a change leader to manage the people side of change. In the 2010s we saw a prevalence of standardised approaches, with training and accreditation to up-skill change practitioners' capabilities.

There has been a trend to manage change in-house with external support used to provide more of a training and support model. Many organisations have invested significantly in building a change practice, however most are still exploring the merits of centralised versus de-centralised models. Internal change practices can find it difficult to balance the strategic change initiative requirements around effecting cultural change combined with the transactional support required on systems and other ongoing change initiatives.

There has also been a recent shift to acknowledge the scope of change programs as transformations of organisations. '*Agile*' is having an increasing impact on how change is perceived and managed. Agile as a philosophy, certainly moves us towards a project implementation approach that supports increased engagement to ensure project implementation success. However, by its very nature of managing incremental changes and history in the software development life cycle it doesn't always cater for the complexities of implementing large-scale, complex, transformational change.

2

The Theory That Fails

The traditional management of Change Approach has been a structured program of activities to understand, plan and implement the change similar to how 'project management' is undertaken. Change is often positioned as a stream of work that sits alongside other project activities, with milestones, schedules and detailed activity plans and resources. This approach does not, however, factor in the very unstructured way that people respond to change. It is very difficult, and near impossible, to predict how much time and focus can be accorded one stakeholder who may be struggling to accept the proposals. One key stakeholder can often have the ability and influence to derail an initiative, and thus, a skilled change practitioner will determine where their work effort is best focused.

In fact, there are as many different responses to change as there are people in the world. Whilst there have been many very helpful ways of categorising and understanding some of the themes in how people respond, they are not a sure-fire way of understanding the many different, and unique, responses that can be experienced by people in periods of change.

In instances where a project has been 'backed-out' or failed to reach implementation, there is disillusionment that 'we had a plan' and the plan failed, resulting in feelings of resentment and loss. At the root of many of these failed changes there are human responses that could have been managed to better prepare for a project of the right size, time, cost, environment and engagement that would have more likely reached its objectives.

A strict definition of project management is one of a sequential, lineal, scheduling of activities to reach a clearly defined end state based on a scoped set of initiatives. The people management aspects of a project are often thought of as an activity to commence when nearing implementation. In recent years there is more of an understanding that people don't '*resist change*', people resist change that is '*done-to*' them, and so a greater focus on early engagement that they can be a part of has been accepted.

Engaging staff early enables them to reflect on what works well that they would like to see retained, allows for staff to raise suggestions for improvement that can then be adopted rather than being told by a new leader or an external advisor on what needs to change. Engaging staff early facilitates their involvement by enabling them to plan their work throughout the program. Thus, they can ensure they have capacity to contribute to the program at the various stages. These contributions could include: helping to compile a list of FAQs required, reviewing documents, validating information and/or work-shopping innovative approaches.

All too often, organisations bring in a change manager when it is too late for this early engagement to occur. They have already scoped where they want to get to, who will be involved and how the outputs will be created, leaving little to no room for staff, the key subject matter experts, to contribute.

The general sequence, in simple terms, is as follows:

1. The need for change is triggered or accepted
2. A leader defines broadly what things should look like and the scope of the commitment
3. A small team of staff work through the hard questions and design a program of work
4. A project team is formed, often including at this point a change manager

These four steps can take anywhere from three to twelve months. In this time, the focus is predominantly on 'where we want to be' (in Transformation[3], this is called the Destination Element). This focus on the Destination Element, can trigger feelings of the enormity of the program. In this typical scenario, the elements of a transformation are already out of balance, this concept will be described in more detail throughout this book. Furthermore, this common practice of establishing programs is fundamentally not in alignment with how things transform.

The change team then commences, identifies why the program team is responding to the enormity of the task at hand, and immediately the change team feels as though it is behind the proverbial 8-Ball. There is a flurry of activity to play 'catch-up' on core activities, including a stakeholder analysis, a readiness assessment and an impact assessment (in Transformation[3], these activities form the awareness element).

Meanwhile, the stakeholders have already heard about this project that has been formed, that they haven't had any input to. They have likely been requested to nominate resources for the team, and/or told what their commitment will need to be. The change team at this point undertake initial consultations to get the lay of the land and instead of having a constructive conversation regarding what the Truth for Change is for each stakeholder and their organisation, individuals have already formed a position and views on their level of commitment and support. They also feel that the Vision, Scope and Direction has been set behind closed doors, without their involvement, and change leaders are back peddling from day 1.

It is through this environment that traditional frameworks for managing change will provide the steps that individuals need to go through to adopt change. They provide a change curve that describes what staff will experience; they also provide a 'plan of activities' but there is no correlation between the two. It is true that if you follow the plan and undertake the communications, leadership, engagement, training and numerous other change activities, people (in the majority) will naturally progress through the change curve and reach the destination.

This traditional approach for managing incremental change however, becomes problematic for fast-paced transformational change initiatives. You often don't have the desired time and resources to meet the full scale and scope of the change activities required. Instead it is more efficient and effective to determine, in the moment, what the needs are and how best to respond. Many of the traditional activities will be undertaken, however they will be done 'at the right time' which will be in direct alignment to address the needs of how the stakeholders are responding to the changing environment. This real-time approach directly impacts the degree of resourcing required, how well people adopt the change, and whether the change meets its objectives.

The Art of How Things Transform

There has been much written on whether change management is art, science or both. There are views that leadership of change is art, and that management of change is science. There are even views that it is neither one, rather being a craft of experienced practitioners. In any case, watching a transformation unfold can be a beautiful thing and to the experienced eye can be a masterpiece.

To achieve a 'beautiful' change, approaches are put in place and adopted throughout an organisation, which provide for a better experience for individuals. Prior to a change program commencing an individual can arrive at an organisation to whispered conversations, gripes, disempowerment, and rumour mills. To then walk through an organisation in it's changed state some 12 to 24 months later and observe new behaviours in action, it can very much feel like a work of art. What the masterpiece looks like is an environment where people re-frame mid-way through their sentences, where executives call out senior managers for not walking the talk (and vice versa), where managers reflect that they have had 'the best conversation ever' with their team, and where the organisation in general is 'lifted', 'energised' and 'engaged'.

Organisational transformations need change management frameworks and approaches in place for change to occur. However, as many leaders have experienced, consultants and change practitioners often come in to build a strategy and plan only to leave the documentation to be implemented by someone else throughout the program. Even where an original plan is implemented there is still a degree of flexibility and skills required to successfully manage an organisation through the transition. This is the real-time diagnostic of where an individual, group, or an organisation is at. Immediately following the identification, is the ability to form a response to 'shift' and move staff forward, maintain momentum and propel them towards the tipping point and into a successfully embedded changed state.

This ability to diagnose how an organisation is responding can be undertaken by an external specialist, but this isn't really a sustainable model, and should really be the role of the CEO and executive team to be able to 'balance' the organisation back into the 'sweet spot' to enable the pace of change to continue in a sustainable manner. Developing this understanding provides a CEO with a 'Secret Advantage' as you will be able to hold your organisation in a continued state of transformational change, to keep pace, and ensure the future sustainability of your organisation.

Change management frameworks, strategies and plans have traditionally followed a three-, four- or five-stage model that is aligned against a project timeline, usually defined along the lines of planning, transition and embedding. Change programs rarely follow this lineal plan in practice. In fact, trying to adhere to a lineal plan can result in doing the wrong activities at the wrong time. The Transformation[3] approach detailed in this, does not replace change management planning; rather, it is an earlier, overarching, more holistic approach for large scale transformations that are aiming to:

- significantly change an organisation
- embed a culture of continuous change and improvement
- build change capability in the organisation

Every organisation has different needs at different times. It is through the 'flexibility' in change management that the greatest transformations can be achieved. It is not a lineal process; rather, it is the identification of the needs of an organisation in transition.

The Transformation[3] model contains three elements (Awareness, Destination, Guidance) that should be equally balanced throughout a program to facilitate the transformation. It avoids the lineal-based approach that can stagnate ongoing benefits realisation in organisations. It also provides for a true culture of continuous improvement by embedding an ongoing, dynamic, real-time approach, that can be sustained post the initial program. This way of managing change is conceptually 'Agile' but in practice can sometimes be even more flexible than some of the Agile practices allow for!

The Transformation[3] model is not a new way of managing change, it captures what is 'actually' occurring when individuals and organisations are transforming, and likely what practitioners have been intuitively facilitating in the 'flexible' aspects of their management of change.

It is reflecting the experiences throughout the transitions in a shared language and framework that can be easily understood by all individuals involved in the change. It assists to align the practical activities that will assist to maintain momentum through to a changed state.

Transforming organisations don't have an 'end date'. The transformation continues long after 'Go-Live', the transition period and the 'Post Implementation Review'.

Activities in a change program send ripple waves through the organisation, they reverberate and continue to reshape and create new ripple waves. If we were to visually depict this paradigm, I'm sure we would again see both science and art reflected in the picture, similar to a visual depiction of sound waves reverberating through different architectural spaces!

It is often quoted that a lack of visible executive leadership support is the number-one reason that change programs fail. Whilst this is commonly a cause of frustration for change practitioners, the lack of visible support is really only the symptom.

The systemic issue in these scenarios is often that a number of the core activities that are required to enable this effective leadership are missing. For instance, there may be:

- an unwillingness to broach a true assessment of the case for change ... which can be more aptly called a 'Truth for Change'
- a vision that is not sufficiently detailed or not in alignment for what is aiming to be achieved
- no plan for getting from A to B.

The root cause of the 'symptoms' that you see when looking at an organisation that is transforming can be more effectively identified when considering the Transformation[3] elements.

In the example provided, where the executive leadership is not as visible as it should be, it is the requirement of the change team to 're-balance' the elements to support the leaders in their sponsorship of the program. Specifically, focusing on the Awareness element will help to sufficiently detail what is and isn't working, aligning everyone to the same storyline or song sheet or understanding of why we are doing, what we are doing.

This message on its own though, would then prompt stakeholders to say: 'So what?' So we then need to also focus on the Destination Element which will assist the leaders to provide a clear and shared vision (informed by and aligned to the Truth for Change). The leaders then need to build confidence in the plan of how we will get there, and this will be informed by all of the activities in the Guidance Element. At this point, you may be reflecting on recent initiatives in your organisation and thinking, *YES! that's exactly what we did* ... which is great, as this balanced approach would have provided a great foundation to commence your initiative.

The Secret Advantage in understanding how things transform however, comes when this great start becomes difficult to sustain.

Understanding 'how things transform' should underpin any methodology or framework to manage people through change. It is this understanding, that is often missing, in traditional change management approaches.

The existing and traditional change management frameworks identify what people experience (for example, denial, awareness, desire, exploration, knowledge, engagement) and what activities to undertake (stakeholder analysis, impact assessment, communications plan), but a direct correlation between the two is often missing. For example, if someone is at any stage along the change curve, the change plan will continue to undertake the activities on the plan, which will shift an organisation, eventually.

Using a real-time approach identifies what people are saying (i.e. *'it won't be successful'*), why they are saying it (i.e. too much in the Guidance Element), which automatically tells leaders how to respond (i.e. here is our plan for successful implementation). Being able to identify this 'in the moment' means you are able to directly respond in the moment, when people are responding to the change (i.e. in a workshop, meeting, town hall, intranet forum) rather than letting all of those individual change responses swirl around the organisation perpetuating disengagement until the right response has been determined.

Most experienced change leaders would have naturally responded to 'it won't be successful' with a reply detailing 'how we will get there' to build stakeholder confidence.

It is an obvious example, however, for less experienced practitioners, or for more complex issues or sustained ambiguity: being able to dissect what you are hearing, why, when and most importantly how to respond can significantly reduce the effort required to make the change successful. Being more efficient and targeted in your management of change not only minimises your return on investment for this initiative but has lasting benefits in how your organisation perceives and adapts to ongoing change.

Using this 'real-time' understanding and approach ensures relevance of the activities being undertaken when they are conducted. For example: it is often the case that a change impact assessment is a moment in time report that gets delivered and then filed in a draw. The Transformation[3] model ensures that the change impact assessment is done at the right time with the right people and that it is re-visited to assist in 'balancing the elements' as required throughout the transition.

4

Big Change Ahead

For the Financial Services Industry, it is clear that there is Big Change Ahead. When considering what these changes may be for your organisation, it is important to be clear on the scope of what will transform before assessing the 'how'. It is particularly important to identify what will be within your span of control and what will be in your span of influence.

Things that are likely to be within your span of control would include planning, knowledge, taking action, relationship management, analysis, skills. Things that are more likely to be outside of your span of control, but within your span of influence could include individual behaviours and commitments, culture, markets, regulatory change, industry trends and external dependencies. This is a simple concept, but it is remarkable how often organisations embark on change with desired outcomes that are outside their span of control. Being clear on this delineation early can alleviate frustrations throughout implementation.

When defining the scope of the transformation in your organisation, consider what your appetite for change is. Out of 10 is this a 6, 7, 8? Perhaps it is a 9 or 10. Consider the effort this will take and the impact on your organisation. Being clear on your commitment to transforming your organisation will directly inform the approach. In the very first instance it will trigger an alignment discussion with your executive team. This conversation will unearth immediate consideration on the scope of the change required and what is with the span of influence and control of the executive.

Detail what a '10' looks like for each aspect of the transformation; services, processes, systems, structure, culture, ways of working. Focus on the aspects of each that are within your span of control. It can be tempting to define a utopian view of the desired destination, but often this requires transformation of aspects that are more within your span of influence than your span of control.

Even if you have already commenced some initiatives, it is worthwhile revisiting them through this exercise, so that they are considered in the context of the broader program of work.

It is worth noting that a critical input to this activity will be the findings of your environmental scanning function. If you have not already established a function of this nature it is highly recommended over this next period of significant change in the Financial Services Industry.

You may also find that it is beneficial to engage staff in

this discussion, encouraging them to provide insights on industry trends and observations into a central repository. By inviting staff to contribute to this process you are opening the conversation on potential opportunities for your organisation and demonstrating that you are open to ideas and suggestions from staff.

The environmental scanning function will be of interest as the outcomes from the Royal Commission continue to effect change in the industry. This will continue for some time as community standards and expectations continue to evolve in response to the new information that has been uncovered and create sustained pressure on FS practices.

Re-set Strategy #1

Ask your executive team:

'What's your/our appetite for change?'

Awareness Element

5

Transformation³
– The Elements

The Transformation³ (T3) Model is primarily built on the 3 elements (Awareness, Destination, Guidance) that should be equally balanced throughout a transformation. The Model is supported by a full suite of materials, including tools, templates and training.

They include: Activities, Skills, Diagnostics, Perspectives, Elements, Leadership, Symptoms and Planning. The 8 Dimensions of T3.

Whilst all of these additional materials and information are helpful, they are not required to begin applying the concept of real time transformation and balancing the elements.

At a high level the three Elements are best described as follows:

- The AWARENESS Element is 'Everything that you have as a foundation to build upon'
- The DESTINATION Element is 'Everything that defines where you want to be'
- The GUIDANCE Element is 'Everything that will help you get there'

The T3 life cycle is infinite: review/respond. Success can be defined at any review point and milestones can and should be put in place so that successes can be celebrated. The model is applicable for any transformation and therefore the framework at its core does not need to be 'tailored', or revised, or defined at the commencement of a new transformational program.

A program does not even need to be commenced for the model to be applied, especially as a diagnostic tool. Observing any individual, community, or organisation will provide an indication of their transformational state. Are they moving forward and evolving/transforming, or are they stagnate, and why? Understanding the Transformation[3] elements is a powerful tool for ongoing management of self and others. There will be times where it will be clearly evident that the Transformation[3] elements are not in balance, and it is by focusing on re-balancing that the movement forward will be able to take place. Think of the momentum of a car with a flat tyre compared to equally balanced and full tyres running smoothly along the road.

Transformations occur in the 'sweet spot', this is the point at which you can say: 'Yes, I have a strong understanding of where I/we am now and all the things that are in place to build upon'. 'Yes, I clearly know and have detailed where I/we are headed', 'Yes, I feel supported in the knowledge, tools, strategies, that will help get us there'. If you find yourself in the sweet spot of a transformation, keep doing what you are doing. Continue to build awareness as things change, continue to define destinations in more detail, or stretch the targets as destinations are achieved. Continue to draw upon guidance that provides new perspectives, tools and techniques. Continue to take action, to review and respond to your organisation as it transforms.

As you learn to apply the thinking around how things transform and balancing the elements, it may take some time to understand which of the activities you are undertaking support which elements. Some activities may fall into more than one element depending on the focus and intention for which it is being performed.

To assist in this process the T3 methodology specifies '*Must Have*' and '*Nice to Have*' activities that can be completed in each of the three elements. The 'Must Haves' are core activities that should be undertaken for any transformation. The 'Nice to Haves' can be undertaken depending on the type of transformation being implemented (in some instances they may become must haves, for instance, Requirements Gathering would be a must have where there is a technology implementation but not as relevant for cultural change). The 'Nice to Haves' provide good options when needing to focus on one of the elements (to rebalance) where all of the 'Must Haves' might have previously been undertaken.

There are a variety of other activities that can be undertaken that lend themselves to enhancing one of the three elements. In fact, all strategic activities that you do as an organisation will fall into one of these three elements.

UNDERSTANDING THE ELEMENTS

Transformations usually start with an awareness of something within the current state that is not working as it should or could. There are many activities that organisations can do to build awareness around the current state. This is the process of considering all the things that are and aren't working. This is stabilising; it gets everyone on the same page. These activities support the 'Awareness Element'. Often these activities are skipped at the start of a program because leaders already feel that their company is stable, or that everyone knows this information.

Then there are the activities that detail 'where we are headed'; these fall into the 'Destination Element'. It is often assumed that detailing a clear-shared vision is not required for staff, as they will only want to know what is relevant to them. Without alignment to the destination, your transformation will head off in many different directions and staff will build their own expectations that won't be met. Be clear on your destination.

Finally, there is the 'Guidance Element,' which gets you from A to B by providing new perspectives and bridging the gap between the current and future states. Without the Guidance Element the gap between where we are and where we want to be is insurmountable. The Guidance Element is not simply 'how we will get there' or 'what we will do'. It includes these things but the 'Secret Ingredient' is the focus on the things that will 'Help' you get there, it is new perspectives, knowledge, assistance, insights. Without these you will continue to address the problems in the same way. A Change may occur, but a Transformation won't.

The Awareness element is the current state – wherever you are in the transition. The current state evolves through a transition, so there is the need to revise the materials created on the original current state. The awareness element is not a moment-in-time activity; it is about constantly looking at where you are in 'present' time. The Awareness element builds upon this understanding of the current state at all levels: for the individual, a group, or the organisation.

For an individual, enhancing the awareness element may be focusing more attention on skills or capabilities that may otherwise be brushed over. For a group, which would include a program or project team, it may be getting everyone on the same page around what works well and what doesn't and for the organisation the awareness element could simply be understanding what is already in place, for example: we use 6 different systems to manage customer relationships.

The awareness activities should effectively document the current state and build a solid foundation for change initiatives throughout the program. The awareness activities should be undertaken throughout the entire program (and beyond) not just at the start. All documentation should be reviewed throughout the program and adjusted periodically as new destinations are achieved.

'Must Have' activities that assist to build the Awareness Element include:

- Stakeholder Analysis
- Impact Analysis
- Readiness Assessment
- Truth for Change

'Nice to Have' activities that assist to build the Awareness Element include:

- Transferable Skills
- Presence and Mindfulness
- Strategic Planning Cycle
- Maturity Model

The Destination Element defines the future state. As the level of awareness increases, so must the clarity of the destination. The Destination includes defining the vision, goals, objectives, benefits, and values. To plausibly acquire a '10', it's necessary to consider not only the span of control and influence, but also the 'balance' and 'trade-offs' to ensure that what is being defined can be achieved within the budget, competing priorities, and resource constraints. The Destination Element details the milestones within the program plan and develops a clear picture of the future destination at points along the transformation journey as well as the final destination desired. The documents that capture the destination, and it's sub-components, should be revised over time and serve as templates for re-use, as future '10s' are defined. They should be transitioned into the business as Business as Usual (BAU) documents, rather than 'project documentation' that is archived.

A good example for Financial Services leaders is to consider the requirement in law to 'do all things necessary to ensure' that you are operating 'efficiently, honestly and fairly'. A strong destination would define what 'efficiently, honestly and fairly' looks like in practice. A strong destination would detail what the benefits of each of these are. It would detail individuals' roles and responsibilities against each and have specific, tangible measures in place that are periodically measured.

'Must Have' activities that assist to build the Destination Element include:

- Benefits Road map
- Vision
- Project Planning

'Nice to Have' activities that assist to build the Destination Element include:

- Creating Culture
- Organisational Pace
- Operating Model
- Organisational Design
- Service Statements
- Requirements Gathering

The Guidance Element bridges the gap between awareness of the current state and reaching the destination. It is the linchpin that provides new perspectives and helps transition the organisation forward. The Guidance Element is supported by independent information and active support.

The Guidance Element is informed by: books, knowledge, wisdom, pulse checks, and surveys. Active support can be provided through leadership, change agents, consultants, mentors, coaching, and facilitation.

'Must Have' activities that build the Guidance Element include:

- Leadership Support Program
- Change Approach
- Effective Communication
- Accessible Engagement
- Strategy Documents
- Methodologies
- Success Stories

'Nice to Have' activities that assist to build the Guidance Element include:

- Empowerment Approach
- Coaching
- Benchmarking
- Case Studies
- Scenario Modelling

There are many symptoms to observe that will provide evidence of the elements being unbalanced. The activities in the 'Must Haves' and 'Nice to Haves' should be selected as these symptoms arise.

There is a full chapter titled 'Balancing the Elements' later in this book which explores the symptoms and activities in more detail. However, in summary:

- Too much attention on awareness will cause the transformation to stagnate, become difficult to move forward, and get trapped in 'the way we've always done things'.
- Too much attention on destination causes the gap between current and future state to become overwhelming causing feelings of lack; in competence, skills, and confidence.
- Too much attention in guidance leads to a lack of ownership; stakeholders therefore 'give power away' and disengage.

It is equally of concern to do 'too much' in any one element than it is to not do enough. The key is to always maintain balance of the elements and this is achieved by the activities we undertake and the objectives and focus we undertake those activities with.

Re-set Strategy #2

Define what 'efficiently, honestly and fairly' looks like, in practice, in your organisation

Destination Element

Section 2
Organisations in Transition

6

The Role of Culture in Transforming Financial Services Organisations

The Royal Commission explored where conduct was linked to culture and whether organisations had attributed this either within their organisation or more broadly in the FS industry. Specifically, the report called out the role that dishonesty and greed played as a driver for the misconduct it was examining.

Whilst organisations may be achieving positive change to their culture, it is worthwhile considering the role of the broader culture of the FS Industry on your organisation. For example, consideration should be made in recruitment practices and the impact of recruiting from a pool of candidates with FS backgrounds which will attract the same ethical mindset. Furthermore, when you do recruit for culture and bring in new talent to challenge the status quo, they must be empowered to do so. In practice this needs to be implemented through an ongoing program (beyond induction) that supports new staff to inject new ways of thinking and operating into the organisation.

Where poor behaviours and decision making have had a spotlight shone upon them, there is a tendency to finger point, lay blame and identify individuals responsible. We accept what we chose to ignore, and in any organisation, decisions are rarely made in isolation. The culture of an organisation creates a space for poor behaviours, and it is the culture that you create that will identify and rectify unethical practices.

I have watched in so many instances where team members ask questions such as 'are we complying with the legislation?', 'does that make us non compliant?', 'are we breaching our obligations?'. Whilst the right questions are being asked the follow-up action and response inevitably comes back to – is that my job or someone else's? Creating a culture where everyone sees this contribution as 'everyone's job' is the only way to ensure that you are sustaining a culture that doesn't tolerate unethical conduct.

When implementing cultural change most organisations will capture some examples of behaviours that are unacceptable (Awareness), they will engage a culture specialist who educate the leadership team on culture and help facilitate a discussion on your desired culture. This invariably results in a set of culture or values statements (Destination) and the specialist may facilitate some supporting sessions with staff (Guidance). The statements remain on the walls/

screensavers and are referred to on occasion until a few years later when they are refreshed, and these activities occur once again. The culture has not been transformed.

The way the culture transforms is by putting the culture into practice in every action. This is achieved through sustained focus on what the culture statements look like in practice. This can be implemented by continually revisiting the cultural statements and 're-balancing the elements'. Provide greater 'Awareness' by capturing what is and isn't working periodically following the launch of the new values. Achieve a more detailed 'Destination' by exploring what the values look like when overlaid over systems, products, processes. Support the gap between what isn't working and change required by capturing the successes along the way (Guidance). And keep looping around the elements with different activities until momentum is achieved and your new culture is owned by staff in everything they do. Most organisations stop at that very first round of culture activities, if that. Quite often only the destination is set, and it is assumed the culture will change by osmosis.

When a new culture is achieved the language will shift from 'we have a value of being ethical' to 'we are a very ethical' organisation.' Consider now, what do staff say are about your organisation?

'We are a very ... organisation.' Proud, Customer Focused, Siloed, Small, Friendly, Dysfunctional, Progressive, Diligent, Process driven? What would you like staff to say?

It is worth mentioning at this point the temptation for leaders to seek anonymous feedback, through 'suggestion box' or survey mechanisms. Not only do I not recommend this practice, I strongly advise against it, as it is counter-intuitive to creating an open culture. Providing an anonymous feedback channel, reinforces that communications in your organisation are 'not open' that people must wait to be asked for their feedback, or, that feedback isn't connected to them as an individual.

Many organisations struggle to create a culture where people feel comfortable 'speaking up'. This can be due to previous negative experiences that staff have had when they have spoken up or it could be 'just the way we do things', your existing culture.

Often, the natural response to this 'symptom' of not speaking up is to provide the anonymous feedback channel as a 'safe' way of soliciting feedback. But at what cost?

Your organisation should celebrate its diversity, its different views and experiences and encourage 'people' to speak up, to own their own views and to build skills and capabilities to frame difficult and sensitive topics in a way that is constructive and beneficial to both the individual, their peers and the organisation as a whole.

Suggested ways to address a culture that is hesitant to 'speak up':

1. Communicate how you want people to engage in the organisation: to be bold, open, inquisitive, thoughtful, proactive
2. Create ways to engage that enable this to occur (i.e. small, informal discussion groups)

3. In large settings, ease staff into the idea of speaking up, rather than asking 'are there any questions' ask 'what are your views, I'm keen to hear your thoughts, comments, views, suggestions' to encourage a more vocal dynamic.
4. If no questions are received, help staff to build the capabilities, provide time to 'discuss any questions with the person next to them', or narrow what you are asking of people so that their questions can't be 'wrong' (i.e. 'I'm really keen to hear what you think about moving our fortnightly activities to monthly, how would this work for you?')
5. Make it fun! It's likely that your staff don't enjoy a repressed environment, make your new ways to engage bright, colourful, light, rewarding and memorable!

These steps equally apply to general engagement and complex feedback scenarios. When you empower staff with the skills around effective feedback, you make it equally easy for them to give feedback whether it is sensitive in nature or not. It is equally important to prepare leaders for 'receiving feedback' as it will be the effectiveness of their response that either enables a culture of feedback or signals to staff 'feedback is not welcome here.'

A final consideration regarding culture is how many FS organisations have recently revised their remuneration practices as a result of the Sedgwick Review. I won't labour the specifics of this issue but there is a big difference between reward and recognition. They are, in fact, two entirely different concepts and should be considered as such.

If someone is capable of achieving significant financial results for an organisation due to being 'rewarded' they are equally capable of achieving these through being 'recognised'. Actually, if you consider Maslow's Hierarchy of Needs, they are potentially going to be more motivated by recognition of their 'self-actualising' efforts, than a financial reward. This of course, is dependent on how well their needs are being met across all categories, but it is worth considering whether you have the appropriate focus in your organisation. Are you creating a space where staff are empowered to deliver their highest value and are celebrated for being all that they can be? What a powerful motivator.

Re-set Strategy #3

Consider what your staff say about your organisation:

'We are a very… Organisation'

Awareness Element

7

Application of Transformation³

We have started to look at the 8 dimensions of Transformation³ by exploring what the ELEMENTS are and what they represent. We have explored the new PERSPECTIVES that this model provides by being in a continual state of transformation. As a Destination is achieved a new Awareness of the current state is formed. People will very naturally go through the change curve, but with consideration of how balanced the elements are, you will be able to target your activities to move them forward with ease:

1. People will naturally gravitate to the elements in alignment with the program phases. For example, people generally start with a good awareness of what's not working

2. Shift them forward by demonstrating 'how' the change can be achieved (Guidance)

3. As the design phase progresses and a Vision or Destination is communicated staff will feel overwhelmed which will cause the 'change curve'
4. The symptoms of the 'change curve' are exacerbated when staff don't take accountability and they bounce between their awareness of all the things that aren't working and a 'big' destination that needs to be achieved
5. Providing Guidance and support assists staff to build awareness of the changed state
6. With new confidence and acceptance, staff explore the destination and how they can contribute to it
7. A strong, aligned focus on 'Awareness' of the new ways demonstrates the transformed state has been achieved.

We have considered the early stages of PLANNING your transformation encouraging the consideration of the spans of control and influence to guide your transformation. In all planning activities whether it be the full program of work, a workshop or offsite, a town hall briefing or even a 1:1 conversation. Consider the content that will ensure that the three elements are in balance. For example, don't launch a program by only talking about the destination, without equally talking about the 'Why' (Awareness) and the 'How' (Guidance).

The next section of the book focuses on the ACTIVITIES that you would likely undertake to facilitate your transformation. Undertaking activities as part of the Trasformation3 model is focused more on outcomes than outputs. There is a reason that you have selected this particular activity, there are objectives that you are aiming to achieve by undertaking it (balancing the elements), and there needs to be consideration of how you undertake the activity to meet the desired objectives. (i.e. there is no point having a report drafted, that doesn't engage staff in the process and sits in a drawer once it is completed.).

Working in sync with your selection of activities is the ability to observe the SYMPTOMS present in your organisation, what are they? why are they occurring? how do you identify them? how do you address them? These questions can be explored through undertaking a DIAGNOSTIC which is the ability to identify how balanced the elements are based on the activities you have undertaken and the symptoms they have caused.

The final chapters in this book look at the SKILLS required to effectively, guide and support organisations that are transforming. These skills include, building confidence and empowerment, framing and reframing and understanding the value of all the unique responses to change you observe. These skills are supported by consideration of the LEADERSHIP role in change. The application of Transformation[3] is completed when we take accountability for the personal role, we all play as change leaders, whether we are appointed into a new leadership position, or commit to playing a change leader role in a transformation or whether we self-manage ourselves through a significant period of personal or organisational change.

8

Understanding the Activities to Undertake

– *What, Why, When and How.*

Transformation³ (T3) is a combination of both what you do, and how you do it. This chapter details the activities that are typically undertaken to support the three elements (Awareness, Destination, Guidance). The activities detailed in this section are not provided as a 'how-to' guide. What this section does provide is a summary of what the activity is, when to undertake it, and what happens if the activity is missing.

This section is for people that like lots of detail. So this will well suit C types in the DISC model or INTP types in Myers-Briggs. It may be too specific for others though and as such, please regard this as a reference section for future use, should you find you need some guidance on what activities to undertake, when and why.

The dialogue in this chapter will help to build capabilities in 'what strong change leaders look for' when identifying 'how balanced the elements are' throughout the transformation and 'which activities to select and prioritise' to rebalance the elements as required.

STAKEHOLDER ANALYSIS

Undertaking a Stakeholder Analysis is part of the Awareness activities in Transformation[3]. This is traditionally the process of identifying, assessing, and devising an appropriate approach for each stakeholder group. It is important to define an appropriate scope for the stakeholder assessment, including consideration of the depth and breadth of analysis. A thorough approach would include meeting with the stakeholders, whereas a light touch model would be desktop-based.

The T3 Stakeholder Assessment activities include an impact/influence tool that analyses findings. The T3 model does not include an analysis of a stakeholder's 'support' for the project, as our experience in leading change demonstrates that when managed well, stakeholder 'support' can shift drastically and quickly. For this reason, it is recommended that when undertaking your stakeholder assessments, do not 'plot' stakeholders support, as this can be counter-productive to a successful transition.

The Stakeholder Analysis is a 'Must Have' activity at the commencement of any transformation to understand the impacted audiences and to devise an appropriate model for engagement throughout the transition. The materials are developed in a way that can be leveraged throughout the program with review points recommended at three monthly intervals. The materials also provide a foundation for other valuable stakeholder activities including engagement heat-maps (a visual representation of your engagement efforts).

If a Stakeholder Analysis is not performed, it is likely that key stakeholders will not be considered in the early stages of the project, which could lead to pockets of resistance within the organisation during the project's transition stages. If the impacts and the influence of each stakeholder group are not appropriately understood, similarly, it can result in a mismatch between the activities undertaken and the needs of staff and managers who are impacted. The stakeholder analysis is a foundation for the change strategy. If it is not undertaken appropriately, the change strategy will ultimately not meet the needs of your organisations stakeholders.

STEPS TO COMPLETE

1. Define scope of activity and tailor approach
2. Desktop assessment of documentation
3. Stakeholder identification and validation
4. Impact/Influence dialogue/rating per stakeholder group
5. Stakeholder approach
6. Recommended stakeholder engagement plan

IMPACT ANALYSIS

An Impact Analysis (often called a change impact assessment) is a 'Must Have' Awareness activity in Transformation[3]. The Impact Analysis informs how the change will be managed. The process will minimise risk, help to think through dependencies, and assist in transition planning. It covers key internal and external impact categories such as: People, Structure, Processes, Products, Services, Technology, Strategy and Operations. The workshops additionally cover the who, what, why, where and how of each initiative, which will assist in communications and 'what's in it for me' (WIFM) scenarios.

The Impact Analysis package in T3 is run as a workshop or series of workshops for each initiative including key stakeholders representing; the initiatives leadership, corporate support areas and impacted operational areas. The outputs of the workshop include an initiative overview, impact rating, impact type, raw workshop notes and an action list for each. The Impact Analysis should be undertaken as early as is feasible in the project – in the planning phase, if possible. However, this factor is dependent on stakeholders having been identified and a fairly strong understanding of the scope of the project, what will be delivered, and where the greatest impacts will be. It is not uncommon as part of the T3 approach to undertake the analysis early and to review and validate the outputs at a later point in the project. This is very much aligned to the iterative nature of the T3 approach, where greater focus in the 'Destination' and 'Guidance' areas will increase the ability for deeper insights in the 'Awareness' activities.

If the Impact Analysis is not undertaken appropriately, risk to the project and to the operations of the business are increased. Similarly, dependencies and action planning may be overlooked, which impacts project schedules and budgets. Transition planning will be inaccurate, causing delays and confusion to stakeholders impacted by the change. An impact analysis can feel as though it replicates thinking performed in the business case or scoping activities of a project. The key difference is that the impact analysis looks to identify 'down-stream' impacts that are best understood by 'end-users'.

STEPS TO COMPLETE
1. Agree depth and breadth of impact analysis
2. Determine Timing of Impact Workshops
3. Develop workshop support materials
4. Agree appropriate representation
5. Schedule workshops
6. Collate output materials
7. Socialise outputs for feedback
8. Agree action plan and ownership of impacts

READINESS ASSESSMENT
The Readiness Assessment is a 'Must Have' activity in the Awareness element of Transformation[3]. It provides an understanding of the enablers and barriers relevant to any project implementation. The Readiness Assessment provides context to ensure that the development of change management and implementation strategies are relevant to the organisations transformation initiatives. The Readiness Assessment is generally undertaken with the leadership

team, project stream leads and managers and can be undertaken in both individual meetings and workshop settings.

Insights are captured around the following themes:

- Aspects of the business that will support success
- Challenges, concerns and risks that may need to be addressed
- What has worked well in other changes
- Communications preferences
- Competing priorities

The Readiness Assessment should be performed as soon after a stakeholder analysis is complete and is practicable. The Readiness Assessment directly informs the design of the Change Approach and ensures maximum efficiency by targeting the 'hot-spots' rather than re-creating the wheel on aspects that may already be highly effective within the organisation.

Resistance to change can be managed most effectively by understanding the individuals, groups and organisation as a whole. The Readiness Assessment is a structured way of identifying what does and doesn't work well when implementing change in your business. The Transformation[3] approach ensures that the recommendations are evidence-based, which cuts through to the core issues that require addressing. This pragmatic approach is proven to target resources and activities where they are most required.

STEPS TO COMPLETE
- Identify proposed audience scope (10-20 ideally)
- Agree Readiness Assessment Approach with Sponsor
- Notify group of pending activity (if required)
- Establish T3 Consultation Database to capture all insights
- Schedule and hold 1:1 readiness consultations
- Code database into readiness 'themes'
- Create summary output
- Socialise and test the themes with the executive/leaders and seek further insights and validation'

TRUTH FOR CHANGE

Truth for Change, more commonly known as case for change or pressure for change, is a must-have activity in the Transformation[3] model. The T3 approach is committed to a humanistic focus that delivers deep insights and lasting change. We focus on a 'truth' for change that empowers individuals and the organisation to capture a realistic assessment of why a change is required. It is through this process that the most appropriate 'destination' can be identified. The Truth for Change is important as the first step in any change program so staff understand why the change is required. The Truth for Change is required at an organisational, team and individual level. The Truth for Change should be 'played back' to staff throughout the change process to maintain momentum. Capturing the Truth for Change is accomplished through multiple channels including desktop review, 1-1 meetings and workshops.

It is important to capture the Truth for Change early in the project to ensure that the scoping and business case activities are delivering against an accurate and well understood reason to change. As the organisation begins to shift, the awareness of the Truth for Change will shift also; because of this, it must be clearly articulated so that it can be used throughout the transition. Generally, you will need to use your Truth for Change when you hear stakeholders saying 'why are we doing this again?'

Change programs often fail to be successfully embedded, and staff return to 'the old ways' soon after an implementation is complete. This is primarily due to the Truth for Change not being well known, understood or accepted and/or what is being implemented doesn't align to what needed to change. The Truth for Change activities empower staff and managers to have 'real' conversations that lead to tangible benefits that can be transitioned to and embedded in the organisation with ease.

A simple activity to test the authenticity of your Truth for Change is to consider the 'case for change' (what's not working in your organisation) and to consider your 'truths' about the organisation (what are your beliefs about how the organisation is operating and performing). Are the case for change and your truth aligned?

STEPS TO COMPLETE
1. Identify how well established the 'Truth for Change'
2. Educate senior leaders on why a strong Truth for Change is required

3. Agree scope of Truth for Change activities
4. Seek a detailed 'Truth for Change' or summary of 'what's not working' at an organisational, group and individual level (workshops, discussions, surveys, activities)
5. Clarify the 'Truth for Change' with senior leaders
6. Consider whether the organisations strategic priorities address the Truth for Change

TRANSFERABLE SKILLS

The T3 Transferable Skills approach is a nice method to have in any transformation as it essentially focuses on people and all they have to offer. Understanding the transferable skills that we have and in particular those that are underutilised is a powerful activity for empowerment and engagement. A comprehensive Transferable Skills undertaking can deliver significant value-add over traditional workforce planning and resource management where there is a focus on 'like skills' that individuals can capitalise upon. Including a Transferable Skills initiative is likely to be of more value in programs that involve restructures and re-defining role profiles.

There is currently a greater drive for life balance for employees, to maximise engagement and productivity. Looking at the transferable skills that individuals have aligns both the interests of the organisation to the interests of the individuals. It facilitates a dialogue for new ways of working, built on empowerment and respect. The approach taken must ensure that each coaching conversation related to transferable skills clearly manages expectations whilst facilitating empowering conversations around the contributions individuals can make to the organisation.

Consider undertaking a Transferable Skills activity when undergoing a transformation, if the company experiences low engagement ratings in pulse surveys, there is anecdotal feedback that staff have many 'untapped skills', there is a need to break down organisational silos, the organisational capability is stagnating, or there is a need for innovative thinking.

There is no risk to a successful transformation if this activity is not undertaken. Maximising transferable skills is a forward-looking approach to maximising your resources. It is the process of proactively identifying the experiences and interests of individuals and leveraging and applying these skills in different contexts. The benefits include:

- greater engagement from employees
- consideration of individuals 'value-add'
- encouraging a culture of innovation

STEPS TO COMPLETE
1. Review engagement results from last staff engagement survey and comments from readiness consultations relating to culture
2. Agree scope of transferable skills activities (range of staff and breadth of skills flexibility desired)
3. Agree how information will be used (involvement in projects/empowerment/cross org networks/communities of practice)

4. Determine and Develop approach for transferable skills activities (individual tools, manager conversations, workshops)
5. Communicate the approach, purpose of activities and benefits for staff
6. Following any activities, follow through on actions, commitments and communicate Success Stories
7. Review and improve on approach periodically as agreed

PRESENCE MODEL

The Presence Model is a 'Nice to Have' in the 'Awareness' element of Transformation[3]. It is an empowerment tool which helps to maximise all of the T3 Awareness activities by assisting participants to be 'present' by building their 'in the moment' physical, emotional and mental awareness. The presence model uses a range of mindfulness techniques combined with the use of our voice and communication skills. The expressive range of the voice (tone, intonation, volume, pace, clarity) provides an avenue to have greater awareness of self and ultimately enhances awareness of others. It is a useful coaching tool when building internal change capabilities and strengthens communication, speaking, presenting and leadership skills.

Consider undertaking Presence and Mindfulness activities when embarking on a large-scale transformation, or conversely; after a period of little or no change. The Presence Model would assist after receiving feedback that staff feel unheard, where there are symptoms of passive aggressive behaviours, where leadership skills are missing (particularly in middle management layers), and when building internal mentoring and change capabilities.

When individuals are 'clouded' by stress, competing priorities, unclear direction or misalignment with an organisation, it can become difficult to lead, support, and facilitate change. The presence model assists individuals to be present in the situation so they can be empowered to make the best choices for themselves and their peers. If staff (leaders and managers in particular) are not present in their own truth, the impacts on a transformation can be that they undermine, sabotage, and resist the change. Where managers are unaware of their own drivers, beliefs and passions, they can be unwittingly contributing to a company's demise. This can occur through believing steadfastly in what had worked at another organisation, drawing conclusions and assumptions without a clear picture or being misaligned with the culture of an organisation, which could be just not a 'good fit'.

STEPS TO COMPLETE
1. Identify drivers for undertaking 'Presence' activities
2. Detail desired and anticipated outcomes
3. Agree scope of Presence activities (Participants and depth of activities)
4. Determine approach (1:1, workshops, paper based)
5. Develop supporting materials/engage facilitator
6. Seek feedback, review and improvement throughout implementation.

Re-set Strategy #4

Consider your own

'Truth for Change'

Awareness Element

STRATEGIC PLANNING CYCLE

The Strategic Planning Cycle is a 'Nice to Have' in the Awareness element of Transformation[3]. The Strategic Planning Cycle helps to solidify how the transformation activities and the existing strategic review and development activities come together.

Change initiatives can often take 3-5 years and can overlap and compete with strategic plans that have gone through considerable development and review. The T3 strategic planning cycle looks at a 10-15 year period that covers strategic planning initiatives prior, during, and after the change. The activity looks at who is involved, who has been consulted and employees' and administrators' levels of engagement into tasks such as annual business planning, 3-5 year strategic plans, independent reviews as well as staff and external stakeholder engagement surveys. The benefits of creating this map demonstrates and ensures cross organisational alignment.

Consider completing a Strategic Planning Cycle Map in large organisations where there are competing priorities, where there is change fatigue from multiple changes over a period of time, or where there are significant regulatory, or external environment changes on the horizon. In any of these situations, preparing a strategic planning cycle map will stabilise and align the organisation to the current changes being implemented.

By the nature of their roles, individuals possess varying degrees of involvement in strategic planning activities. In change programs, it is important for staff to know where they have been, where they are, and where they are headed.

It satisfies both the 'Security' element of Maslow's Hierarchy of Needs and also contributes to the 'Self-esteem' and 'Self-actualising' needs, as staff can see how they have contributed and where they will contribute in the future. Remember, people tend to resist change that is 'done-to-them,' so it is important to enable staff to 'shape the change', or at least demonstrate where and how they contribute to this process.

It is important to note that staff length of service is often significantly longer than leadership positions. Employees will remember their tenure in great detail, especially the failed initiatives and hollow promises. Be on the front foot and acknowledge where they have been, what they have been through. Be clear on the future planning initiatives and what involvement they will have in shaping the future. A future which may well be beyond the length of an executives contract (but not outside the span of influence for an inspirational leader!).

STEPS TO COMPLETE
1. Undertake desktop review to create a timeline of all past and planned strategic planning initiatives for 5 years prior and 5 years forward looking
2. Detail how each planning activity took place and who was involved
3. Socialise and Validate the Strategic Planning map
4. Communicate to relevant stakeholders and use to develop background materials and context for the change as required.

MATURITY MODEL

A Maturity Model is a 'Nice to Have' in the 'Awareness' element of T3. Maturity models can be performed against established industry benchmarks or, performed against an agreed internal organisational criteria. The maturity model is formed by undertaking a series of consultations, supplemented by a desktop review of materials. The maturity model is a foundational document for any transformation. Oftentimes executives feel that they have a strong understanding of the maturity of an organisation and this activity is skipped over (keep an eye on how well balanced your elements are, you may want to revisit this activity). It is common that 'quick wins' are identified from this process, simple improvements to operations that would significantly contribute to the success of a transformation if addressed early (for example, identifying and removing double handling will generally be a big win for staff).

Maturity Models are undertaken ideally prior to establishing a project, as they assist to understand the weaker elements in an organisation and can shift priority areas prior to undertaking transformational change. Maturity Models are a 'Nice to Have' in a transformation as they provide a strong foundation for the Truth for Change, but are not always critical (albeit they are highly recommended). An organisation could already have a strong understanding of the Truth for Change, which could be informed by a previous independent review, a regulatory, policy, or service change and it is therefore not always required. However, the risk of not undertaking a maturity model across all facets of the business could mean that the transformation is not addressing critical issues that could undermine the success of a transformation.

STEPS TO COMPLETE
1. Determine whether maturity assessments have been undertaken previously
2. Agree Maturity Model approach including using a particular model or devising bespoke
3. Agree scope of functions being assessed
4. Develop criteria for assessment (if required)
5. Undertake assessment (desktop, 1:1, workshops)
6. Develop maturity assessment report
7. Validate report and use as an input to determine 'Truth for Change' and 'Desired Destination'

A Benefits Road map is a 'Must Have' in the Destination Element of Transformation[3]. Benefits road maps, which are traditionally captured in project management methodology, detail what, and by when, business benefits will be achieved through undertaking project activities.

Change management strategies traditionally play a role in ensuring that benefits are realised. Benefits realisation activities should ensure an actionable approach – that is, stakeholders are proactively contributing to the benefits throughout the change. Benefits are not realised by osmosis. Tools and templates should capture goals, accountabilities and milestones providing transparency and alignment to address aspects identified in the 'Truth for Change'.

The development of the benefits roadmap should be undertaken early in the project's establishment, detailing to a granular level, anticipated benefits identified in the business case. The benefits roadmap should be further refined throughout the transformation through engagement activities such as leadership action plans, Case Studies,

Success Stories and client feedback. The benefits roadmap should be tracked periodically and re-aligned as the other elements shift.

In traditional project management methodology, it is assumed that once realised, the project scope will ensure that benefits are achieved. However, this is often not the case, as change impact analysis activities often uncover that there can be multiple operational business dependencies that can impede benefits realisation if not undertaken simultaneously.

STEPS TO COMPLETE
1. Ensure program of work is sufficiently detailed to undertake benefits mapping
2. Detail at a high level, the anticipated benefits for the entire program (5-10 high level, but specific benefits)
3. For each high level benefit, detail with a number of related and more granular benefits
4. Ensure for each granular benefit, that an accountable person is assigned, that regular milestones are detailed against the program timeline
5. Develop a visual communications tool to demonstrate the from/to for each benefit and the road map throughout the program
6. Regularly communicate progress against the benefits realisation road map.

VISION

Undertaking vision activities describes 'what will the organisation look like' once the change is complete. It is not an organisations mission statement, or an aspirational reflection on what the organisation would like to look like. A Vision Statement is specific, achievable, and time-bound across all aspects of the transformation (consider span of control and influence here too).

Detailing the Vision to this level of detail assists to focus everyone who is contributing to the change to the same goals resulting in an efficient use of resources working in a coordinated manner to achieve the anticipated benefits. The Vision is informed by any activities performed in the 'Awareness' element. The more thorough and detailed the 'Awareness' activities have been the more you will be ensured of a strong Vision Statement.

The Vision Statement is a must-have in any change program and should be done early in conjunction with 'Awareness' activities such as the Truth for Change, Maturity Model and Strategic Planning Cycle. The Vision and Benefits roadmap are also closely linked providing a 'check and balance' against what is achievable. It is not uncommon to undertake the development of a 'high-level' Vision Statement with the detailed information available following the completion of other T3 activities.

In the context of change programs *'often failing due to a lack of visible executive sponsorship and leadership'* the Vision activities ensure the executive team are aligned and communicating the same destination. Facilitating a clear-shared vision enables leaders to lead the organisation through the transformation. Without a Vision Statement for the change, leaders may inadvertently misinterpret and miscommunicate what is aiming to be achieved. This can ripple through all levels of an organisation, causing confusion and resistance to change.

STEPS TO COMPLETE
1. Desktop review of literature, strategies and plans to identify where the organisation has considered and communicated how it would like to operate in the future.
2. 'Play back' aspects of the desired destination to senior leaders to prompt further discussion, detail, clarity and alignment
3. Identify gaps in the development of the Vision and devise plan to solidify thinking (workshops, activities, 1:1, benefits road map, external guidance)
4. Capture agreed Vision on a Program on a Page that covers the who, what, why, when, how to achieve the desired destination

PROJECT PLANNING
Effective change management is critically dependent on sound project management being in place. If governance, scoping, schedules, roles and responsibilities, risks and issues and all associated Project Planning documentation is not appropriately and effectively developed and managed, any change management activities will be rendered pointless. Where project management is missing the change management efforts will be re-allocated to establishing project management protocols being established prior to continuing with the change effort.

In T3, Project Planning is a 'Must Have' activity in the Destination Element. It is an audit, establishment, education and alignment activity, and ensures that the selected project management methodology and artefacts meet the needs of the specific transformation being undertaken. It also ensures that there is alignment between the project team and impacted stakeholders. Purist models of project management methodologies (whether you are using Prince 2, Agile, Waterfall or others) can be ineffective if project staff and impacted stakeholders have different levels of experience and understanding of the stages, activities and materials in use in that specific methodology.

The Project Planning audit, establishment, education and alignment activities should be undertaken when: it is a large scale transformation, there is not strong experience of project management in the organisation, the project team are external to or new to the organisation, the steering committee are not clear on, or confident, in the project management approach, there is discomfort in the organisation regarding the transformation, there is distrust in the organisation (vertically or laterally), and/or there is a silo culture across impacted areas.

When project management processes and artefacts are missing, the confidence in the project team can be diminished. Impacted managers and staff can harbour resistance to a change if they have concerns on how the project is managed. If there is sound project management in place it should be communicated for transparency and inclusiveness. If there are project management aspects that are missing, or not working, engaging with stakeholders on their preferences and requirements is a powerful collaboration and engagement exercise. Communicating what the project management approach in place is, does not need to be an exhaustive process, a 'one-page' summary of what is in place and what can be expected of the project should suffice.

STEPS TO COMPLETE

1. Assess Consultation database for insights on how effective and well established the project management approach is
2. Identify gaps in the effectiveness of governance, scoping, schedules, roles and responsibilities, risks and issues
3. Socialise gap analysis with program sponsors and program team and identify plan to address areas of concern
4. Communicate key aspects of Project Management approach to build confidence for stakeholders and to ensure that roles and responsibilities are clear and agreed

CREATING CULTURE

Creating Culture is a 'Nice to Have' in the Destination Element of Transformation[3]. Not every change implementation will require a cultural change; however, cultural alignment to what is being implemented is fundamental to a successful change. For example, implementing a new system may not in itself impact on the culture of an organisation, but implementing a system that is in conflict to the values or 'the way we do things' will require a cultural alignment activity to ensure its success.

The T3 Creating Culture approach recommends maximising any transformation to refresh and renew the ways of working in an organisation. Focus on culture can create momentum and improve staff engagement.

Including T3 Creating Culture as part of a transformation can be a far more effective and efficient way to affect cultural change than as a stand-alone program. It is recommended that a Creating Culture element be included in every transformation, which could span from a cultural alignment activity to ensure implementation success to a full culture change initiative. Creating Culture is informed by the Truth for Change, Maturity Model, Readiness Baseline, and Vision.

The more management and staff that are involved in Creating Culture activities, the more successful the broader program will be. Creating Culture can and should be focused at individual, group and organisational levels. If a cultural focus is missing in a transformation, the change can be unsuccessful, as it may not be adopted or used in the way intended (for example, staff may use the new system, but they do so in a way that is disrespectful to their colleagues).

If there is a cultural misalignment the risks to the projects success are increased. If a cultural change is desired but there is not a dedicated cultural change initiative, it is unlikely that the culture will change or change in the desired way. Transformations in themselves can affect the culture of an organisation (for example staff may lose trust in management); therefore, it is important to ensure that any culture that is created is a positive experience for staff.

STEPS TO COMPLETE
1. Agree 'appetite' for cultural change with program sponsor
2. Capture cultural activities undertaken in the organisation in the 3 years prior
3. Assess consultation database for cultural observations
4. Keep a log of cultural observations from floor walks, and experiences, capture examples and be specific on what's observed
5. Include a 'cultural session' in workshops/off-sites as appropriate to gather further insights
6. Summarise the top 5-10 high level cultural areas of concern, validate with senior leaders
7. Detail culture statements that explain what the desired culture looks like in practice
8. Devise program of work to socialise the culture statements with staff and seek individual commitments to work in new ways.

ORGANISATIONAL PACE

Organisational Pace is a 'Nice to Have' in the Destination Element of T3. Organisational Pace is a comparative analysis and an assessment and recommendation of the appropriate pace for your organisation. The pace is considered for both throughout the transformation and the pace for your operations as a BAU organisation. Having the experience of working from one organisation to another both within and out of transformation initiatives provides the ability to review the strengths and weaknesses of an organisations pace. Too slow and momentum is lost, pettiness sneaks in, over-engineering simple activities occurs and staff manufacture job security. Too fast and burnout and absenteeism occurs, strategic thinking gives way to just getting the job done and having time to consider working smarter is all but a dream. The assessment of pace looks at all levels, functions, and groupings across the organisation to assess and identify the optimum pace. The optimum pace then aligns leaders and managers to tailor transformation initiatives accordingly. As an example, when staff talk of change fatigue it can sometimes just mean 'tired', staff have sustained a pace that has been too fast for too long.

Most organisations will not have a strong awareness of their organisational pace. Anecdotal feedback can be misleading, as it is comparative to internal and recent experiences. It is recommended to undertake a T3 Organisational Pace review when undergoing a significant transformation, where there is, or is risk of, change fatigue, where there are competing priorities, where there is a disconnect between the anecdotes, workloads and perception. Indicators in the organisational pace analysis include: attendance and punctuality, responsiveness to correspondence, presence and attentiveness in face-to-face settings, bespoke solutions, 'creating' work and offers of assistance. If the Organisational Pace analysis is not undertaken, some of the underlying issues in an organisation can be exacerbated in a change program and could reinforce unhealthy behaviours and ways of working.

STEPS TO COMPLETE
1. Assess your consultation database for comments relating to capacity, duplication, creating work, workload and other themes that inform a sense of the pace of the organisation

2. Capture examples, being specific on what's observed
3. Assess at an organisational and group level where the pace lies comparatively to other organisations
4. Socialise the outcomes of the rating activities with the executive team and discuss appetite for change in the organisational pace
5. Develop plan of work to address gap between current and desired organisational pace
6. Seek feedback throughout, Report, Review and Improve

OPERATING MODEL

The development of an Operating Model is a Nice to Have activity. An operating model is a conceptual picture that shows how the parts of an organisation should work together. It can be designed for a particular function or for an entire organisation and the level of detail can range from a straw man to full operational guidelines. Operating models differ in organisations; therefore, the T3 operating model focuses on a significant scoping activity to ensure that the designed operating model meets the needs of the organisation in transition. The development of an operating model covers considerations such as people, processes, services, systems, structure, support, strategy, facilities, locations and environment and is usually best developed in a workshop setting.

The development of an Operating Model should occur early in a transformation but requires input from 'Awareness' elements. The development of an operating model is a good pre-cursor to organisational design, as it shifts participants' thinking into an organisational and shared view rather than 'where do I fit in the structure'. Operating Models should be undertaken when there are silos, where there is not strong awareness of all of the parts of the organisation, where collaboration is missing, where things are 'thrown over the fence', where there are inefficiencies in the operation of the organisation. The benefits of developing an operating model increases awareness, collaboration and focused efforts within an organisation.

If it is missing, an organisation can feel as though 'the right-hand doesn't know what the left-hand is doing'. This can be problematic when most organisations have five to eight major limbs! Duplication, spinning wheels, and inefficiencies are likely outcomes when an operating model is not clearly defined, documented and communicated.

STEPS TO COMPLETE
1. Agree with the executive team, the purpose of undertaking an operating model activity, is it strategic, conceptual and/or operational in its desired outcomes
2. Develop an agreed approach for the scope an activities to develop the organisations operating model
3. Collate inputs
4. Develop Straw man – with or without leaders input at the drafting stage (as agreed)
5. Socialise Straw man, refine and build out full detail
6. Devise implementation plan

ORGANISATIONAL DESIGN

Organisational Design in Transformation[3] is a 'Nice to Have'. Not all transformations require structural changes that involve a detailed organisational design approach. The T3 approach to organisational design is an inclusive engagement approach that identifies what is working well and what isn't in the existing structure through assessment activities such as a SWOT analysis (Strengths, Weaknesses, Opportunities, Threats) for each area.

Organisational design is invariably a process of trade-offs. For example, groups that sit together are more likely to collaborate and maximise their synergies whereas multiple groups that will require to be assembled together generally aren't feasible. These instances can be managed through matrix and networked models; however, there will always be trade-offs. Impacted managers and staff will be far better equipped to manage themselves through any structural change if they have been part of the design conversation.

An Organisational Design activity should be undertaken when: the degree of structural change required to support a change is not quantified, the executive have identified some changes desired, but they are not yet concrete or have not been communicated, previous structural changes have been 'done-to' staff and have received poor feedback and/or the size of the organisation will be impacted (note: degree of engagement in this instance will be limited). The benefits of structural change are realised in 'the way that people work' within the new structure. It is therefore pertinent that people understand why they have been structured this way, what the benefits are, and how they are expected to work differently. If the organisational design activities are not undertaken, staff will not transition to the structure smoothly, it will likely not be a feasible or appropriate structure and it likely won't deliver on the anticipated benefits.

STEPS TO COMPLETE
1. Agree appetite for structural change from the executive
2. Determine whether it is anticipated that there will be a reduction in head count
3. Agree level of engagement with staff to design structural changes
4. Develop approach and timeline for organisational design activities

SERVICE STATEMENTS
Service Statements are a 'Nice to Have' in the Destination Element of T3. Service Statements are complementary to the development of an Operating Model and Organisational Design and/or can be developed as stand alone documents as required. Service Statements are an internal communication and awareness activity to assist other parts of the organisation to understand: who we are, what we do, when to come to us, what to expect (including any SLAs). The T3 Service Statement approach is very much a facilitation activity so that there is full ownership of the Service Statements by each group.

Service Statements can be developed at any time either through a transition or during BAU. Service Statements should be considered when: staff are not aligned within a function, staff are not aligned across functions, there is duplication, ownership and accountability issues, new functions and groupings are being implemented, there is a reluctance to collaborate and work across areas. As an example, the FS Royal Commission identified confusion on roles and responsibilities as one of the core issues emerging from their Case Studies. Specifically this was with regards to intermediaries, however, was also evidenced by some of the larger financial services organisations being unable to effectively compile information from their organisation in an efficient manner.

Service Statements are a 'Nice to Have' output, but they are a relatively simple and effective way to facilitate better collaboration within and across groups. If there is a misalignment between what a group feels is the service they provide and what is expected of them, the operational effectiveness can be impacted. The more coordinated and consistent the Service Statements are across the organisation, the easier the information will be available and understood by all staff. The cultural aim through this initiative is: 'Everyone knows who to go to and what to expect'.

STEPS TO COMPLETE
1. Determine timeline for service statement activities (time post org changes as appropriate)
2. Agree scope of service statement activity across the organisation, i.e. to what level?
3. Develop the organisations service statement templates
4. Determine approach to develop Service Statements with areas (workshops/facilitated, etc.)
5. Ensure consistency across all Service Statements and publish in easily accessible way

REQUIREMENTS GATHERING

Requirements Gathering is a 'Nice to Have', as not every transformation has a technology component; however, if there is a systems element to the transformation, Requirements Gathering is a critical activity. Oftentimes there are wasted resources on design and build activities that could have been avoided with an appropriate and inclusive requirement gathering approach. In programs with long development and lead times, the T3 approach recommends checkpoint reviews of the requirements with business owners to ensure that any changes within the business are being addressed. i.e. I couldn't tell you how many times I have assisted programs to be implemented where a leader says 'I wasn't here when they did the Requirements Gathering. I would have asked for different things.'

Requirements gathering should be done early in a transformation that has a technology component. It will be dependent on a number of 'Awareness' and 'Destination' activities as Requirements Gathering needs to be in the context of the program and not an open wish list of unrelated requests. It is critical that a Stakeholder Analysis be undertaken prior to Requirements Gathering so as to ensure appropriate participation in the discovery conversations/workshops. If Requirements Gathering is not done at the right time with the right people, in the right way, the project team will likely not build a solution that meets the needs of the organisation. Even where the mandate is clear for the desired requirements, it is important to have a detailed conversation with end users to ensure that seemingly insignificant requirements are captured. This step will assist in the adoption of the solution and can often result in manual effort and inefficiencies being avoided.

STEPS TO COMPLETE
1. Develop an understanding of past Requirements Gathering activities and their approach (capture what worked/didn't)
2. Agree scope of Requirements Gathering activities
3. Agree audience for Requirements Gathering sessions
4. Ensure materials are prepared that clearly articulate the context, vision of the program, anticipated outcomes of system improvements
5. Ensure approach is communicated so that all staff are aware of when and how Requirements Gathering activities are taking place
6. Socialise outcomes to participants (and broader audience as agreed) for further feedback
7. Clearly and regularly communicate how and when requirements will be delivered

LEADERSHIP SUPPORT PROGRAM

A Leadership Support Program is a 'Must Have' in the T3 approach. Leadership support activities ensure people in leadership roles are positioned for success, and ensure transformations are meeting their objectives. Activities include individual meetings to develop leadership capabilities through a leadership action planning process. This process includes engagement preferences, roles and responsibilities assessment through a RACI (Responsible, Accountable, Consulted, Informed) benefits realisation action plan, and cultural commitments. A report is provided to the executive capturing commitments made. The Leadership Support Program is best supported by a regular forum for leadership development.

The Leadership are generally (and ideally) considerably involved in early scoping activities and 'Awareness' and 'Destination' workshops and conversations. The leadership role becomes more 'real' once the program is communicated to staff and managers and leaders are expected to cascade messages and answer questions. The best timing for the commencement of the Leadership Support Program will likely fall between the planning and transition phases of a project.

If a Leadership Support Program is not in place, it is common for managers without strong change leadership experience and skills to fail to manage their staff through the transition. The Leadership Support Program ensures consistency in the support, messages and approach across groups whilst facilitating and supporting individual leadership styles. Transformations without strong leadership at multiple levels of the organisation may fail to achieve the desired change.

STEPS TO COMPLETE
1. Determine scope and approach for the Leadership Support Program
2. Develop Leadership Action Plan Template
3. Review best time to commence Leadership Support Sessions in the context of the broader program and change plan
4. Schedule and hold sessions
5. Capture all insights into the consultation database
6. Code themes, analyse information and create de-identified summary report of leadership plans for the executive sponsor to demonstrate progress and areas that require addressing

CHANGE APPROACH

A Change Approach is a 'Must Have' in T3. The Change Approach provides a coordinated way for managing the transition. It clearly articulates what is required and why and provides a baseline for measuring the effectiveness of the change program. The Change Approach draws heavily on other aspects of the T3 elements including Truth for Change, Vision, Leadership, Effective Communications, Accessible Engagement, Cultural Alignment and Success Stories. The detailed development of the Change Approach into a Change Plan for your transformation details the types of activities that should be undertaken for each including planning, analysis, tools and templates, face-to-face sessions, documentation and communications.

The Change Approach should be completed in the Planning stage of a project following the completion of baseline documents such as the Stakeholder Analysis, Readiness Baseline and Vision Statement. The greatest value of a Change Approach is the communication of the approach to the project team, leadership and impacted staff as it builds confidence and aligns all stakeholders to a consistent approach.

The Change Approach is a 'Must Have' document that becomes vital through the transition phase where change can become 'hard'. Having an agreed, endorsed approach for the change can minimise the instance of resistance. Change can often be misunderstood as simply providing communications. This misunderstanding alone can result in staff feeling that a change is being 'done-to' them, implementing a Change Approach that is purely one-way communication will rarely result in a smooth or successful transition.

STEPS TO COMPLETE
1. Determine the core components of your Change Approach, drawing on insights from your consultation database
2. Detail what each component of the Change Approach looks like in practice and the anticipated outcomes when it is well established
3. Ensure that your Change Approach provides a mechanism for ensuring the Transformation elements are balanced (activities in all three transformation elements)
4. Detail the Change Approach against the project timeline which will develop into the change plan which details what the activities are, when they will be undertaken who will be involved and how they will be undertaken
5. Build the change plan into the overarching project schedule and complete and report on tasks accordingly

EFFECTIVE COMMUNICATION

Effective Communication is a 'Must Have' in T3. Effective Communication identifies all the existing channels in a coordinated manner including the creation of a 'team meeting map' across an organisation. Effective Communication leverages preferred channels from the T3 Readiness Assessment and identifies which existing channels can be leveraged and which new channels should be established. An operating rhythm for communication channels is developed and templates for new communication channels provided.

Effective Communication should be established early in the program following the identification of stakeholders and completion of the Readiness Assessment. It is a 'Must Have' in any transformation and should be completed in consultation with existing internal communications resources.

If the T3 Effective Communication activities are not completed, a change program can find that messages are being delivered to the wrong people at the wrong time in the wrong way. Often a 'cascading' approach (an expectation that leaders at all levels pass messages on to teams) is assumed but fails to communicate effectively – damaging the reputation of the program and ultimately the successful adoption of the change.

STEPS TO COMPLETE
1. Review your Consultation Database for insights into how effective current communications channels are
2. Agree scope of 'change communications' and any overlaps dependencies with internal communications
3. Identify existing communications channels that provide a platform for change communications
4. Capture a list of all the 'pieces of information' that require communicating and consider their origin, author, channel, frequency, importance and any supporting templates
5. Plot the information along the timeline for the program/change plan
6. Socialise the Communications Plan with stakeholders to build confidence

ACCESSIBLE ENGAGEMENT

Accessible Engagement is a 'Must Have' in T3. Engagement is often something that is 'provided', but often not 'received'. If staff have been through multiple changes where they feel that the change is 'done-to' them, they tend to assume this change will be the same. It can take multiple forms of engagement for staff to realise that their views are wanted, they will be listened to, and they will be responded to. The Accessible Engagement approach is about understanding the barriers to engagement in an organisation, which could include capacity and permission but oftentimes stems from a lack of trust. Making engagement accessible is about identifying the existing engagement channels and auditing their effectiveness, including coverage of preferred learning styles within your organisation (understanding your organisational pace will assist here too).

Accessible Engagement should be undertaken early in the program following the identification of stakeholders and completion of the Readiness Assessment. It is a 'Must Have' in any transformation and should be completed in consultation with existing internal communications resources.

If Accessible Engagement is missing, staff impacted by the change can harbour previous experiences of change throughout the transition resulting in delays and resistance. It can also mean that staff with vital knowledge to the design aspects of the transformation are not contributing through the development phases, which results in a solution that is not fit for purpose. Project members will primarily have a 'focus to deliver', which can often be at the detriment to a successful change. Performing Accessible Engagement activities early will mean that project members have a suite of channels on hand to easily engage, socialise and test what is being developed.

STEPS TO COMPLETE
1. Assess the current levels of engagement in the organisation
2. Review the consultation database for identified barriers to engagement (individuals, attitude, past change, culture)
3. If completed, look at the pace of the organisation to identify capacity for engagement activities
4. Review the Program Plan and identify activities that would most benefit from staff involvement
5. Look at the operating rhythm of the program and plan ongoing and ad hoc ways to engage

STRATEGY DOCUMENTS
Strategy Documents are a 'Must Have' in T3. Strategy Documents are clarifying and confidence building. They align all project stakeholders on the agreed strategies to support the transformation. Strategies required will vary depending on the type of transformation being undertaken, and can range from conceptual design to strategic planning, from transition strategies to operational strategies. They include objectives and goals and timelines and draw together context and focus areas, scope and principles. The T3 approach to strategy development is a clear definition of the scope and purpose of the document up front and facilitation of effective conversations and desktop review to inform the strategy development.

Strategy Documents should be undertaken on an as-needed basis but should be completed and endorsed before activities to implement them are underway. Consider the development of Strategy Documents where the organisation is embarking on activities that are new, there are differing views on the purpose and approach of initiatives, or where there are multiple input sources.

Strategy Documents keep things 'on-track.' This is particularly important in any change program when the transition phase can be difficult. However, it is easy to lose sight of what was agreed in the planning stages of a project. 'Scope creep' (where new aspects are added to the project late in the piece) can often occur as impacted stakeholders become more engaged and foundational documents such as strategies become powerful tools for keeping the project moving forward. This is not to say that added scope should not be considered, rather, that it be managed in the context of the strategies and plans that have been put in place.

STEPS TO COMPLETE

1. Identify where there are capability gaps in the organisation and agree what functions require a strategy that covers the Principles, Objectives, Goals, Focus Areas, Scope and Timelines
2. Agree a consistent format for Strategy Documents as appropriate
3. Meet with the executive sponsor to agree scope and purpose of the document
4. Utilise all existing inputs such as the consultation database and literature reviews to inform the development of the strategy

5. Socialise a draft of the strategy to ensure alignment
6. Seek formal endorsement of the strategy
7. Reference your Strategy Documents frequently throughout your transformation
8. Communicate the strategy or aspects of the strategy to stakeholders to build confidence

METHODOLOGIES

Methodologies are a 'Must Have' in the T3 approach. Methodologies are agreed ways of undertaking aspects of an activity and can include quantitative and qualitative techniques. A methodology provides a system of methods that draws on research, previously tested approaches and frameworks for thinking.

Methodologies may be established industry standards that are being adopted by an organisation or an organisation may require a methodology for a particular aspect of their organisation such as project, governance, process, or change management methodologies.

Methodology development should be undertaken to standardise the frameworks for thinking in an organisation. Where there has been significant change or staff turnover, different frameworks can undermine progress where there are differing views on how to undertake activities. Many methodologies are similar 'but different', and often a facilitated conversation can help align language and approach and develop a shared framework to progress initiatives.

Methodologies eliminate assumptions in how transition activities should be approached. If the methodologies for project, governance, process or change management are not agreed, aligned, and consistently applied, the project risk increases.

Being clear on the 'how' is equally important as the 'what'. It also increases project risk to have an agreed methodology being applied, that is not understood or not followed by all stakeholders. A pragmatic approach to clarify and communicate agreed methodologies, can minimise the instances in projects that feel like 'going around in circles' or 'going nowhere fast'.

STEPS TO COMPLETE
1. Use your Truth for Change to identify where there are gaps in the effectiveness or stakeholders' understanding of how effective functions are
2. Identify whether the function(s) have a clear approach that is based on research and best practice in the field
3. Consider what 'off the shelf' methodologies there are and whether they are applicable and meet the needs of the gaps identified
4. Buy, outsource or develop methodologies as required
5. Ensure there is a clear executive summary of the key aspects of the methodology to ensure alignment of stakeholders within the organisation to the agreed method being adopted

SUCCESS STORIES

Success Stories are a 'Must Have' in T3. They reinforce changing behaviours and are a powerful guide for staff in the midst of transition to demonstrate the benefits of the change. Success Stories also provide organisational leaders with a 'pulse-check' on the success of the change and once the stories peak and subside are a strong indication that a comfortable BAU state has been achieved. Success Stories are created by staff who are in the transition. Capturing Success Stories in the right way can be challenging for staff who may not have reflected on their work in this way previously or are not as yet clear on the benefits of the change.

Success Stories should be captured from the earliest instances of pilot and transition activities. Success Stories should be undertaken in the first instance by change champions who should be in place 1-2 months prior to transition activities occurring. Any change program can be undermined by a lack of confidence in the change and the benefits being realised. Success Stories are tangible examples of how the new ways of working can be a positive experience for both individuals and the operations of the organisation. If stories are not shared, it is likely that resistance to the change may linger with sentiments such as 'it won't work', 'we've tried this before,' or 'the new way is harder than it was before.' These comments quickly reduce when peers demonstrate that they have made a successful transition to new ways of working.

STEPS TO COMPLETE
1. Communicate to stakeholders at all levels the need for Success Stories to help move an organisation in a transformation to the transitioned state

2. Agree an approach for capturing and communicating Success Stories
3. Agree the behaviours or ways of working that you want to celebrate the achievements against
4. Consider other activities occurring within the organisation along the program timeline and when the best point to start capturing Success Stories is
5. Develop an agreed Success Story template. Establish a central repository for Success Stories that draw out the headlines and link to the full story (SharePoint lists are a good way to achieve this)
6. Communicate to all stakeholders: what stories to capture, how to capture them and why they are important
7. Set targets for leaders and change champions to collect Success Stories and celebrate when targets are reached.

EMPOWERMENT

Empowerment is a 'Nice to Have' in T3. The T3 Empowerment Approach is a process of working with individuals to identify barriers in their professional environment and developing strategies to address the barriers and realise their fullest potential.

The Empowerment Approach strategies can be a transformational activity for an individual in itself outside of an organisational change. This approach focuses on 'self-awareness' and 'professional destination' supported by a coaching approach.

Organisations may wish to offer Empowerment sessions for individuals who are undergoing a transition to refresh and re-focus to support the transformation. This 'Nice to Have' activity can deliver significant results. The Empowerment Approach should be offered to staff; this approach should not be targeted to individuals and there should be no mandatory participation. Empowerment conversations can be confronting, and individuals need to sign-up for the process. If staff are disempowered, there will be a reluctance to perform tasks, productivity may be low, and staff may select the tasks that they want to perform, rather than those that need to be performed. Staff may be highly productive but on the wrong activities and may not be aligned to the organisational direction. Often these instances are considered poor performance, but the underlying barriers are not addressed. Barriers to strong Empowerment could include lack of accountability, recognition, opportunity, diverse work, capability development, contribution and satisfaction.

STEPS TO COMPLETE
1. Agree scope of the Empowerment activities with the executive
2. Identify some of the organisational barriers to Empowerment, and what is aiming to be achieved through the Empowerment approach
3. Develop a plan for the Empowerment approach activities based on the agreed scope, ensure that the activities provide an avenue to rate: How empowered I feel? My perception on barriers to being more empowered? What my working life would look like if I felt more empowered? 'My empowerment commitments: I will ...'

4. Capture individuals' insights and commitments and summarise in a de-identified report
5. In alignment with the agreed approach, follow-through with individuals to ensure commitments are complete and capture benefits and Success Stories of improved ways of working

COACHING

Coaching is a 'Nice to Have' in T3. Coaching helps individuals to identify, discuss, reflect on and address aspects of their professional interactions that are not working at a '10'. The 'running at a 10' concept focuses on items that are within an individual's span of control and can remove blockages and perceived obstacles significantly improving engagement, efficiencies and quality of performance. Coaching sessions can be general in nature or to assist with specific areas of concern.

Providing a Coaching component is recommended in any transformational change. The design of the 'Guidance' component in T3 facilitates enhanced 'Awareness' and defining 'Destinations' and providing support to bridge, and assist, in the transition. A Coaching component can be provided at any point in a transformation, or BAU environment, however, the most effective timing to provide Coaching sessions is after a program launch in the preparation stage for transition. If individual Coaching sessions are not provided as part of a transformation, long standing, and often easy to resolve barriers can remain. A transformation program is a good 'trigger point' to confront items that can impede professional development. If Coaching is not provided, personal concerns about the program can impact individuals' support for the change and the ultimate success of the program.

STEPS TO COMPLETE
1. Discuss with the executive, the anticipated benefits of Coaching and scope of activities
2. Determine whether the Coaching program will be an in-house informal 'buddy' model or an external, independent professional coach arrangement or a hybrid model somewhere along that spectrum
3. Regardless of the approach taken, ensure that the activities are coordinated, and clearly communicated (as appropriate) to ensure a fair approach for all
4. Regardless of the approach undertaken, ensure that individuals are encouraged to reflect upon and share where there have been positive outcomes as a result of the Coaching activities

BENCHMARKING

Benchmarking is a 'Nice to Have' in the Guidance Element of Transformation[3]. Benchmarking is when organisations look at an external comparative analysis of their activities in a particular field. Analysis can be performed against established industry benchmarks, or performed against an agreed internal organisational criteria. Benchmarking can also be performed using internal knowledge of external practices, which can be a powerful way to leverage internal knowledge and experience, which in turn, empowers your staff.

Benchmarking activities should be considered when there are external drivers for a change or when there are concerns against practices not meeting industry standards. Benchmarking is often undertaken when new leadership brings in expertise from competitors prompting a review of internal practices. Benchmarking is most beneficial in the early stages of a project's initiation.

Benchmarking is a 'Nice to Have', and therefore is not a critical activity to an internal transformation. Benchmarking activities can ensure alignment with or advancement ahead of comparative industry practices. Without Benchmarking activities, it can be difficult to discern value-add over competitors or point of difference in the market. Benchmarking is recommended for Financial Services organisations over the next 3-5 years as competitors implement changes as a result of the Royal Commission.

STEPS TO COMPLETE

1. Refer to 'Awareness' activities undertaken (such as the Truth for Change and Maturity assessment) to inform where Benchmarking activities may be required
2. Identify where there are open questions in the Operating Model or Organisational Design and Benchmarks may be useful
3. Agree scope of Benchmarking activities
4. Identify whether a formal Benchmarking service or Methodology is desired or whether informal in-house data gathering will suffice
5. Source data in the agreed categories and compare to internal information
6. Provide the benchmarking report to the executive for consideration and assistance in agreeing the desired destination

CASE STUDIES

Case Studies are a 'Nice to Have' in the Guidance Element of T3. Case Studies are a structured review of individual activities and provide valuable insights on consistency, approach and improvements. They can be applied to any work scenario and are not limited to work considered as 'case management' as can be the default approach in some organisations. Case Studies include coverage of the who, what, why, when, how and provide a holistic view of activities undertaken. Capturing Case Studies in a structured and consistent manner provides for deep analysis of practices.

Case studies can be undertaken at any point in a transformation, they can inform the Truth for Change, or capture instances of the destination already in practice. They can also be instructional for staff in transition. Consider undertaking Case Study activities where there is a lack of visibility, where there are inconsistencies in approach, when needing to draw out specific examples, both positive and negative. If Case Studies are not undertaken, it can be difficult to discern actual practices from perceived practices. Often staff believe there is consistency, or they are undertaking work in a certain manner, yet when left to interpretation, outputs can vary significantly. Within a change program, performing Case Studies can improve the quality of and degree of change achieved. They can be a good way to re-visit a previous change if there is uncertainty on how well the change has been embedded.

STEPS TO COMPLETE
1. Determine purpose for capturing Case Studies
2. Determine scope of Case Studies required at all levels and functions or a limited area

3. Agree template and inclusions covering the who, what, why, when, how of the activity being reviewed
4. Determine approach for capturing (autonomous, workshop, facilitated. 1:1)
5. If appropriate, house in a central repository
6. Use the Case Studies to inform the 'Truth for Change' as appropriate

SCENARIO MODELLING

Scenario Modelling is a 'Nice to Have' in the Guidance Element of T3. Scenario Modelling minimises risk by 'playing out' scenarios of concern when it comes to transitioning to new ways of working. This activity will be beneficial to Financial Services Organisations as Environmental Scanning won't necessarily identify what other organisations 'will' do over this next period of significant change. Scenario Modelling can provide a foundation for testing design aspects throughout the transition and can assist stakeholders to understand what is being proposed. Agreeing parameters of the scenario modelling prior to commencement enables focused activities with minimised impact to subject matter experts.

Scenario Modelling should be considered where the change is complex, cutting over multiple parts of the business, or uses an unprecedented approach in the organisation. Scenario Modelling scope should be agreed as early as possible in a project and outlines should be created as part of 'Awareness' and 'Destination' activities wherever possible.

If Scenario Modelling is not undertaken, it is likely that assumptions will be made based on previous experiences.

Scenario Modelling opens outside-the-box thinking and can inform decisions that are more fit for purpose and aligned to likely organisational outcomes. Scenario Modelling helps to align stakeholders on the same page, the risk of not undertaking this activity is where key project and business leaders are working to a set of different assumptions.

STEPS TO COMPLETE
1. Identify, through program governance channels, the need to map likely scenarios related to transitioning to new ways of working
2. Detail the parameters of likely scenarios and their outcomes
3. Undertake a risk assessment of likely outcomes
4. Agree preferred approach
5. Re-visit scenarios modelled throughout the transition and adjust approach accordingly

If you have worked your way through all of the activities and detail in this chapter, you may be feeling as though there is a significant workload required to undertake these activities. To alleviate any of these concerns, I can assure that managing change effectively is not by doing 'more' it is absolutely about selecting the right activity, at the right time, and undertaking it in the right way so that the objectives are met. This section is intended as a guide and provides general advice on how to undertake the activities. As part of the full Transformation[3] methodology, tools and templates exist for each of these activities and in most cases, they can be completed in a way that minimises the impact to an organisation whilst ensuring the objectives of the activity are met.

Re-set Strategy #5

Review your Environmental Scanning practices.

Guidance Element

9

Balancing the Elements

As was introduced earlier in this book, the fundamental understanding of how things transform is the ongoing balance of focus between the three elements (Awareness, Destination, Guidance – have you memorised these yet?). Ideally, by the time you've finished reading this text you will be naturally seeing the elements in your everyday life, be identifying where there is 'too much' focus in one of the elements, the symptoms that are occurring as a result, and what activities to undertake to get things back in balance and moving forward effectively!

This activity of balancing the elements is achieved through a diagnostic. A diagnostic in this model can be a thorough and formal process, a quick yes/no response to a series of questions, a manual assessment of where the current focus is, or very simply in conversation with someone, listening to their language and description of current status, feelings and responses. This chapter will explore all options to effectively diagnose your organisation in transition.

A full, formal diagnostic of your transformation program is not always required. Whilst there are a range of options that will suffice, in some instances a thorough option will provide the ability to re-set the program, re-engage stakeholders and build confidence to progress forward. A full diagnostic includes a desktop review of work undertaken, stakeholder consultations and a comprehensive report providing recommendations for the following period of work.

The most common diagnostic undertaken for organisational transformations is the yes/no question set. An online version of this is available at www.transformation3.org which provides an open access Diagnostic Assessment Tool and Report. It has been developed to assist organisations to assess weak points in their transformation approach and is best completed when you are already underway with some form of change or transformation initiatives. It can, and should, be completed periodically to ensure the elements remain balanced as you transform.

A more simplistic version of this tool can be manually performed by looking at each of the activities in the elements (see Chapter 5 for the listings) and scoring yourself a '2' for each 'Must Have' and a '1' for each 'Nice to Have' activity that you have undertaken. Totalling your score for each element will provide an indication of whether your focus has been balanced, or which elements may need more attention to help maintain momentum through your transformation. Include any additional strategic activities that you have undertaken in your organisation that may fall into the three

T3 elements, this will also build your understanding of the types of activities that you are already doing, and how they are providing momentum in your organisation.

Undertaking a Diagnostic 'in conversation' is one of the most enjoyable, enlightening and beneficial ways of applying the transformation thinking. By simply asking someone 'how are you tracking?' and allowing them to talk, you will hear what they have done and how they are feeling. As you become more proficient in applying the model, in real time – you will see the correlation between the activities they have undertaken and will know exactly how they are feeling as a result. This will occur before they even share any insights on the current symptoms, they, or their stakeholders are experiencing. To practice the thinking in your next workshop, steering committee or executive meeting try to identify 'which element' each person is currently in. This will be evidenced by the activities that they have recently completed, the challenges they may be facing and/or the type of engagement they are experiencing with their staff.

As you begin to apply the model, you will observe as I have, that whilst the model is straightforward on the surface and occurs naturally in so many everyday situations (where people naturally seek guidance and so forth to help them move forward) that our responses in an organisational setting tend to be counter-intuitive to 'how things transform'. If we start undertaking Awareness activities and something stops moving forward people tend to choose more Awareness activities, because they were the conversations that helped us move forward in the first place. Similarly, we may have set a Destination for the future which created energy amongst stakeholders, then as the energy dispels leaders step in with more about the Destination – further putting the elements out of balance! Likewise, I am sure that anyone working in public or private sector organisations has witnessed a situation where a myriad of external consultants are brought in to solve a problem, this cycle can occur for many years and is exacerbated every time you 'seek guidance' from elsewhere, without taking accountability internally. Hopefully, of all the content in this book this paragraph has resonated with you the most and has demonstrated for you just how important it is to apply this understanding of how things transform to your role as a leader.

The following section will assist you to rebalance the elements by detailing the symptoms that you will observe or may be experiencing if your focus and activities are not equally balanced across the three T3 elements. It also details what you may experience if you undertake any form of diagnostic and score low in any, or all of the elements.

THE AWARENESS ELEMENT

If your company rated low in the Awareness Element, you may not have spent sufficient time focusing on and capturing where you are now in the current state. Programs are often formed under the assumption that everyone is trying to fix the same problems.

Focusing more attention on Awareness elements will:

- help align all stakeholders with the same understanding
- identify things that are already working well that you want to keep
- show you what truly isn't working and why

- help you address the biggest issues first and manage dependencies better
- identify duplicated effort in your organisation
- prepare you for a smooth and effective transition

If you rated moderately in the Awareness Element, you have likely undertaken several activities already to understand, document, and socialise the current state. You have also undergone a significant amount of preparation to understand who needs to be involved, and when and how to progress your transformation successfully.

You have a strong understanding of who will be affected by the changes and you have considered the readiness and preparedness of your organisation to change. You need to consider additional activities in the Awareness Element if there is more focus on the Destination and Guidance Elements.

If you rated highly in the Awareness Element, you are well prepared and know the importance of planning and building a strong understanding of your organisation and the changes proposed. However, if you are higher in the Awareness Element than in the Destination or Guidance Elements, you could find that your program gets stuck. Too strong a focus on where you are currently without also balancing your attention on where you are headed can feel like you are spinning your wheels.

Too much attention on the Awareness Element may lead to the transformation stagnating. It may become difficult to move forward and be easy to get trapped in 'the way we've always done things'.

Symptoms of being 'too much' in the Awareness Element include:

- Feeling 'stuck'
- Being aware of all the problems and no solutions
- 'Complaining' – not enough detail, movement, or action
- Loss of momentum – quick starts the fizzle
- High energy dropping to low energy

Remember that throughout the transformation it is important to acknowledge that the current state evolves. It is necessary to continually revisit and revise your Awareness Element, especially if symptoms of being 'too much' in the Destination or Guidance Elements are arising.

THE DESTINATION ELEMENT
If you rated low in the Destination Element, you may know where you're headed, but haven't specified the details sufficiently to align and guide project activities. Detailing the Destination Element to greater depths occurs throughout the transition. However, the more detail you can capture, and provide sooner, the more effective and efficient your transformation will be.

Focusing more attention on Destination Elements will:

- ensure everyone is headed in the same direction
- avoid duplication and recreating the wheel
- ensure your project management approach is efficient and effective

- remove cultural barriers to achieving your vision
- ensure that your destination can be achieved by maximising the pace of your organisation
- build awareness around how each part of the new organisation will operate
- ensure that what you are building, designing or delivering meets the needs of your organisation

If you rated moderately in the Destination Element, you have likely undertaken a number of activities to detail what the future state will look like. However, you may have failed to sufficiently detail the design of the 'downstream impacts' of your implementation and/or sufficiently communicated the future state to all impacted stakeholders.

Your program is most likely progressing towards the desired destination; however, there may be a disconnect as you move closer to go-live. This would occur if the Awareness and Guidance Elements are not also sufficiently progressed. This will be evident if/when stakeholders are asking Why? and How?

Conversely, if the focus becomes too weighted in Awareness and Guidance, you will find that there is a drop-in momentum, in which case it will be pertinent to detail the next level of specificity of your future state.

If you have rated highly in the Destination Element, you know where you are headed in a great level of detail and have likely communicated this well to stakeholders. You understand the downstream impacts and have planned for what they will look like and how to get there.

Be mindful that if there is too much attention in Destination, the gap between current and future state becomes overwhelming, and there may be feelings of lack, that the road ahead is long, hard and unattainable. It can feel exhausting if your organisation is too focused on the destination without acknowledging where you are, how far you have come and how successfully you've achieved changes to date.

Symptoms of being 'too much' in the Destination Element will include:

- Feeling overwhelmed
- Loss of control, too much happening too fast
- Uncoordinated, inconsistent approaches
- Cultural misalignment – throwing out the good with the bad
- Not sure what problem you're trying to fix
- Questioning 'whether it's worth it'

THE GUIDANCE ELEMENT
If you rated low in the Guidance Element, you may be planning a lineal trajectory from A to B, but should be considering whether this is the right path and the right way to get there? The Guidance Element ensures that there are significant support channels and outside influences to test, validate, check, align and to ensure consistency, quality, support and delivery against your Vision.

Focusing more attention on the Guidance Element will ensure:

- momentum is maintained throughout the program

- impacted stakeholders have an opportunity to 'shape the change'
- there is strong leadership at all levels of the organisation to assist in the transition
- that there is a culture of continuous improvement established
- that change capabilities and resilience are built throughout the implementation
- that the change is successfully embedded
- that the anticipated benefits are realised

If you rated moderately in the Guidance Element, you have probably completed a significant amount of activities to support your organisation through the change. You have invested in supporting and developing leadership capabilities in your organisation and have detailed the 'how' to ensure that you have a smooth transition.

You have most likely tested your approaches to a moderate degree to ensure that you are aligned to industry benchmarks. You seek external guidance, knowledge and support to ensure that you are doing the right things in the right way. You have a good understanding of possible scenarios as a result of your implementation and have planned your response to each.

If the Awareness and Destination Elements are greater than the Guidance Element, you may feel that the program gets stuck, or there is a 'lack of confidence or trust' in what is being implemented and how.

If you have rated high in the Guidance Element, you are likely committed to doing the right things in the right way and you are well prepared and have planned for the transition. You understand your internal and external environments and have considered alternative models and are confident in your approach.

The Guidance Element bridges the gap between the current and future states. If there is too much attention in Guidance compared to Awareness and Destination, there may not be effective ownership. This means key stakeholders may be 'giving power away'; they are possibly not taking accountability and leading the change.

It is understandable to have a larger Guidance Element early in the project but could be a warning sign if you have rated highly in this element and are struggling to get traction in your transition.

Symptoms of being 'too much' in the Guidance Element will include:

- Lack of accountability
- Feeling that the change is being done to you
- Overuse of consultants and outsourcing
- Lots of strategies, frameworks and guidance documents but no action or outcomes
- Feeling 'disconnected' from the change – it's happening 'over there.'

WHAT TO DO WITH YOUR DIAGNOSTIC?
Validate your assessment. Whichever diagnostic approach you take, once you have a sense of the elements being out of balance, continue to validate the assessment and develop a deeper understanding of what is occurring and why. Is it

shared across stakeholder groups or are different pockets out of balance in different ways and for different reasons? Yes, it starts to get complicated. Balancing the elements is not an exact science, as soon as you identify where something is out of balance, it may naturally shift in another direction. This is the key aspect of it being a 'real-time' model to assess and respond. By simply asking someone 'have you undertaken a …' or 'do you understand the …' you have already planted the seed that shifts their focus and 're-balances' them.

Section 3
Skills for a Secret Advantage

Re-set Strategy #6

Undertake a

Diagnostic.

An online tool is available at:

www.transfromation3.org

Guidance Element

10

Creating a Space

The following chapters provide insights on 'the how' of managing transformations. This is where there is often more 'art' than 'science' when managing people through change. There are not always formulas to apply along the way; experience will guide the best approach. The skills provided will be more important for executive leaders and specialist change practitioners leading transformational change, but the principles can be equally applied, and scaled for all levels of change support and leadership.

→ *Relinquish any personal need for control or validation.*

This cannot be stressed enough. It is a fact of life that we are drawn to certain roles and experiences based on our own 'life journey'. However, a need for control, or a need for personal validation and success can be completely destructive to a change program or transformation. A facilitator of change with a need for control undermines the principles of empowerment, involvement and acknowledgement, aspects that are critically important for those impacted by the changes.

Having a change leader who is 'in control' is different to one that needs control. Different stages along a change journey require different attributes from their leaders and so it is important that those leading change are able to run the full gamut of 'control' as it will change significantly throughout the program. At the start of a program it is likely that the change leader will have a very significant span of control and influence and should be able to confidently take the reins where required.

However, as the change leader facilitates empowerment and ownership, they will need to adapt and relinquish control in the hand-over to internal resources and management structures. At this point, there should be no personal drivers for a change leader to maintain control, rather it is a point to develop influencing skills and move into more of a supporting role.

Seeking personal validation as a facilitator of change, similarly, is counterproductive to facilitating change. The key mantra for any external resources to internal resources should be: 'How can I make YOU successful?'. This is also a powerful tool in a reverse hierarchy, where a senior leader may empower their direct reports by relinquishing any need for control with this phrase/commitment.

An indicator that there is an issue here will be where project, change or internal resources say, 'my project, my budget', etc.' They have a personal attachment to the outcomes, not a collaborative one. They are attached to the outcomes because it feeds personal validation.

→ *Be clear on your professional values and what they look like in action*

Leading change can often be an isolating paradigm. As either an internal leader driving change, or an external specialist facilitating change you can often feel as though you are swimming against the tide. It is important to have strong grounding within yourself around your motivations and your actions. Most organisations have a set of values and are leading initiatives internally to ensure that employees are living them.

However, what happens when the change required is different to the existing set of organisational values or are unrelated to the change you are trying to create? Just like any change methodology, without this cultural direction and alignment, it is likely that what you are trying to implement to some degree will be unsuccessful.

Simple solution = Create your own set of values

The following set of values, I created when working with a number of different companies simultaneously. I devised these values when working on client site, engaged through an executive recruitment firm, via a resourcing company, alongside a consulting firm, into multiple organisations. The values at one of the clients were externally focused facilitating an internal cultural change.

Confused?

Yes, so was I. I created a set of working values for the engagement and they have become a valuable tool guiding all of my professional interactions and to 'measure individual performance' through multiple engagements.

- Build strong relationships
- Be a positive representative
- Provide deep insights
- Create a space of trust
- Deliver value

Whilst the majority of readers of this book will be executives in ongoing roles, the objective is the same. Consider your professional values and how they support the organisations objectives. Are you sustaining values from a previous organisation? From your personal life or involvement in community groups? How do your professional values need to be applied to support the organisation to achieve its objectives? Are your personal values and those of the organisation not aligned at all? (My apologies if you have just answered yes to this question, it will be difficult not to be aware of this now!)

→ *Consider the type of space you are comfortable creating*

If we consider the ladder of inference, where we are all a product of our experiences, it is fair to assume that we are all therefore comfortable in different types of environments. Consider the types of spaces you are comfortable in and how that translates to the types of spaces you create for your staff/team/peers/organisation.

Today, we are far more adaptable in our choice of environment. We are aware of the difference that a colour palette can make for our mood or the ability of 'greenery' to transform an office space. We are also becoming more aware of the emotional space that we create with our words and our intentions. This is the idea of 'creating a space'. Setting an intention, such as openness, and communicating this intention, supported by an appropriate room setting.

A facilitator (internal or external) will often be fastidious on the scheduling and time management of a workshop or forum, and in many instances, this is the 'space' that is required: time and delivery focused. Other times, a facilitator will seem to meander around time, with thoughts and activities allowing a natural flow of conversation to occur, this too may be exactly what is required.

A space to contemplate. There are many different spaces that are created by facilitators. This section is not a 'how-to guide' for the various tasks and myriad of tones that create different spaces; rather, it is an encouragement to think about your own adaptability across spaces that you might create. These spaces will be in direct alignment with the personal and professional values you uphold in all your interactions.

For example, creating an emotional space where people are encouraged to be open about their feelings requires a level of sensitivity and skill to be able to manage the full range of responses that may eventuate. Would you be comfortable calling out comments that could be construed as personal attacks in a professional and respectful manner?

Would you be comfortable supporting someone to release emotions, enabling them to feel supported and not judged by other participants in the session? Would you be competent to effectively re-group a session if someone responds against a proposal and walks out in anger?

Consider the types of spaces you are creating. Oftentimes, to find ownership for a change, individuals need to experience their responses to it. The more experienced the facilitator the more 'processing', accountability and ownership of individuals responses to change will occur. Similarly, however, creating a space that you are not equally able to manage, can be detrimental to individuals experience of change and their future adoption and engagement in change initiatives. In these situations, some specialist assistance may be required.

→ *It's not about you*

People's responses to change are not about you. They are their responses, based on their experiences and the onus for managing these responses is on them. Your role, as a leader or change facilitator is to create a space that enables people to have their responses, manage themselves through it (with appropriate support and guidance) and adopt the changes required of them. Similar to a need for validation or control, check that you are not overly invested in others' emotions – this is an unsustainable approach that neither helps them or you.

Similarly, external support resources, whether they be project, change, or other specialist practitioners should never be seen to have a personal view on the changes an organisation should be making. This is for a few reasons. External resources are there to facilitate an outcome, which largely relies on the engagement of stakeholders.

It is therefore very difficult to build trust and confidence in the engagement mechanisms if stakeholders feel that their contributions will be 'filtered' and misrepresented. Stakeholders can feel that an external resource would never have the same depth of knowledge that they do as an SME in the business and therefore will be reluctant to allow their views to be fed in to the process if they feel there are ulterior motives at play.

It becomes instead about aligning the contributions to the Vision, the Desired Destination that the project is trying to achieve. This points to the imperative of having a clear shared vision, well documented to sufficient detail so as to enable influencing conversations where a change leader or facilitator can steer a conversation towards the Destination that has been set by the executive. This can be done through effective questioning and exploring what the Vision could look like in practice. An ability to constructively challenge scenarios that are presented and ensure alignment to what is aiming to be achieved.

This is not to say that external advisors cannot provide guidance, advice and expertise on best practice, based on their experience and knowledge. It is purely a reminder that an external resource should not have a 'personal' investment in the outcomes in a way that prevents internal resources from taking accountability and adopting the change. Internal and external resources working on changing an organisation often find themselves in significant positions of influence, working directly to executives on acceptance and commitment. This organisational positioning is critical to the effectiveness of successfully embedded transformations and should be treated with respect.

→ *Role model reframing and positivity:*

There is a long-held view that change management is the process for communicating to stakeholders. This is one important aspect of change, but change doesn't occur through communications it occurs through conversations. Conversations provide stakeholders with the ability to share their views, comments, questions and concerns and for a change leader (which could be a CEO, manager, external facilitator or a peer) to respond in a way that enables that person to move through their response and adopt the change.

Always…

- Thank participants for their time (also acknowledge if you are aware that people are under the pump)
- Provide an overview of the agenda and ask, 'is there anything else people were hoping to cover today?'
- Check whether the information or session was useful and/or met people's needs
- Encourage views, thoughts, responses to be aired, it is much easier to manage them out in the open in the room than passive resistance or negative responses on the rumour mill
- Acknowledge every contribution as a positive and valuable one; every response helps us to review and improve.

Positivity and negativity are equally contagious, approaching every conversation or activity with positivity, will offset a lot of the negativity, that people may bring with them in periods of uncertainty.

→ *Value down – Value up*

It is an interesting dynamic in relationships where two people do not feel as equals. The responses can be that an individual tries to 'pump themselves up' to feel more equal or to 'take down' the person that they feel inferior to. Whilst this section is not on the psychology of equality, there is merit in considering whether you are a 'value-up' type of person or a 'value-down' by default. Organisations that are transforming, invariably unearth 'power-imbalances' as people will gain confidence in the change at different times. Stakeholders may have concerns regarding their skills and capabilities. The change may require them to think and behave in a different way which is challenging to them.

This concept of value up, value down is the idea of deflating energy versus adding to it. Some people add value by criticising others, their ideas and approaches. Whilst the critique may lead to a better outcome – at what cost? This 'value-down' approach is unfortunately very common in hierarchical environments. It doesn't, however, lead to empowerment and inclusiveness, which are vital in a successfully adopted change. The more constructive approach is 'value-up' where you add value by taking what's already there as a foundation and building upon it. It's perfectly okay to disagree and provide the required critique and feed, but there are respectful ways of doing so and you will create a significantly different space if all views are valued.

Re-set Strategy #7

Consider your own

personal drivers

Destination Element

11

Framing in Change and Transformation

Framing is important to ensure that the right 'tone' and intention surrounds the communication of change. A quality change management function in your organisation will ensure, based on their knowledge and experience, how change should best be communicated. Your change function cannot however filter every communication (for example Q&As, informal conversations etc.) to ensure that it achieves the right objectives. A very simple example of this would be: 'I've decided I want you to do it this way' compared to 'thank you for your suggestions, based on your feedback we will review this process so that we can all work consistently in an efficient manner'.

The following points are a general guide of the common 're-framing' edits that are made in communications regarding impacts to staff.

US/THEM/WE/YOU/OUR/YOUR

The use of us-and-them language can be a subconscious trigger in individuals where they feel excluded or segregated or that something is being done 'to-them'. It is important to select the scenarios in which you use this language carefully, some common considerations:

- Avoid this language when talking about formal processes, such as determining someone's position (i.e. the org design process rather than our org design process). Also ensure language reflects that the approach has been the same for everyone.
- Avoid when talking about decisions that have been made, for example, replace 'we've decided' with 'a decision has been made, based on consultation, your feedback, our strategy to…
- Use 'we' when there is a personal element, for example: 'We sincerely appreciate all the effort that has occurred to reach our destination'.
- Use 'our' when something is shared, for example: 'our organisation', 'our processes', 'our culture'.
- Avoid 'our' when the information is exclusive, for example: 'our approach in making this decision' should be 'the approach in making this decision'.

These are guidelines more than rules, reflect upon the language you are using and the sense of inclusiveness you want to create. Consider the impact of your language, which will have downstream consequences to empowerment and engagement.

POSITIVITY

- Use positivity when talking about positive approaches, processes and engagement, for example: 'It is exciting to see how many responses have been received'.

- Don't use positivity (be neutral and factual) when delivering messages on what's changed or changing; staff may not feel as pleased about the changes as the executive to begin with. Rather, align the messages to previous messaging on the Vision, for example, 'In alignment with our aim to deliver services to customers quicker, a process is being implemented to streamline our approach.'

- Avoid 'We are pleased to announce' unless the change is a positive change for all staff and there is no ambiguity in the change, i.e. 'We are pleased to announce all staff will receive a 10% pay increase on 1 January' is acceptable, 'we are pleased to announce we're restructuring' is not.

ACKNOWLEDGMENT

- Always acknowledge where there is ambiguity and uncertainty in a balanced way; do not make assumptions that it is the only response, for example: 'We are pleased with the levels of engagement and conversations occurring about the changes and acknowledge that for some people ambiguity over the detailed changes can be difficult'. I constantly hear leaders say, 'change is hard' it may be for some people, but not all, by saying this you are creating a culture of 'change is hard for us'.

- Always include rationale regarding why there is ambiguity and uncertainty as part of the process. For example: 'We are keen for staff to be part of the process to 'shape the change' and as such, we don't currently have all the answers'
- Always acknowledge staff involvement in the process to date, for example: 'As we discussed with staff throughout last year…'
- Always acknowledge the building blocks in the process, for example: 'Following on from our communication last year, last month, last week…'

TIMELINE AND DATES

- Always provide a high-level summary of what activities are planned to be occurring when
- Always provide key dates and milestones when they are 100% locked in and going to occur
- Provide anticipated timelines where the need arises, use soft language to demonstrate the date is aspirational, for example: 'At this point', 'most likely', 'aiming for', 'anticipate', 'expecting to have'.
- Be mindful not to communicate specific dates that may not be achieved. Significant trust will be lost if commitments are broken.
- Do communicate where there are dependencies so that staff understand the activities that need to occur, and why something may take longer than staff may want.
- Do communicate what staff should do along the timeline to engage until more details are known.

- Do 'name the changes' if an aspect of the change is not given a brand it will, by default, be labelled by its date. For example, 'We will advise staff at a meeting in June' will become 'the June meeting' and you will be held to this date.
- Do communicate a broad timeline as early, mid, late in a year until this can be more specific. Staff will push for a month. Hold the line until you are 100% certain it will occur. Rushing strategic changes to meet dates can result in an unconsidered, rushed, poorly thought through and executed change.
- Do distinguish between what staff 'want' to know, and what they 'need' to know, for example a manager may need to know more specific details to plan team resourcing.

Some ambiguity (Chapter 15) can be an important tool in facilitating new ways of working. A few unknown elements, such as specific dates can create a space for exploration. Again, these are points for consideration that will require tailoring to the specific situation of your transformational environment. I have witnessed many change programs fall off the rails because of one simple miscommunicated message, always test your messages and language wearing a 'staff members hat' prior to sending.

12

Successful Change Builds Confidence

Successful change programs take people with them on the journey; they do this by building confidence. The word 'confidence': ORIGIN *late Middle English: from Latin, confidentia, from confidere meaning 'have full trust'.*

If we very simply consider the things that enable staff to be 'full of trust', herein lies one of the most important aspects of successfully managing change.

Ask yourself the following questions...

- Do you have a dedicated 'face of the change' that builds confidence in the approach? (Sponsor, Product Owner, Transformation Director, Change Lead)?

- Is your change manager (or equivalent*), capable, organised, confident and a natural leader?
- Are the change and project documents professional, well presented and accessible?
- Does your transformation program make achievable commitments and follow-through on commitments made?
- Are staff confident that they will be heard, that concerns will be considered, are they confident that the organisations values will be adhered to throughout the change?
- Are your lead project and change resources and their teams perceived as competent, intelligent, capable, respectful, inclusive, engaging?
- Are your key change and project leaders and executive sponsor aligned and supportive of one another, working to the same plan, from the same song sheet?
- Are your transformation resources working to a primary objective of your organisation realising its vision (as opposed to the very common 'securing more work' paradigm. Change resources in particular, should be confident enough in their abilities to make your change, and their stay with your organisation the shortest possible time)
- Are your project and change resources motivated by 'your success', not 'their success'? (An indication here is if they refer to the change as 'my program')

---

* The term change manager is used to describe the person accountable for leading a change, this could be a transformation or change lead, director, senior manager or manger. This differs to the broader term of change leader, who are all the individuals facilitating and supporting the change, without necessarily holding specific accountability for managing people's responses to the change.

- Are your change facilitators genuine, likeable, authentic, open, building strong relationships, and are people who you are ... *confident you can trust*?

Top tips for building confidence through periods of change:

Consistency – Establish operating rhythms for forums, channels and messages early and stick to them. Do not re-schedule, cancel, deem not worth it, change audience, exclude, un-invite, miss, fail to be organised, not send agenda, not send record of meeting following. Do always ensure you are punctual, inclusive, regular, reliable, consistent, welcoming, explanatory, organised, prepared.

Polished Presentation – Documents should be branded, include links to further information and contacts. As above, there should be consistency in the visual elements and format and inclusions of the documents. People are far more likely to trust the information if it is presented well. Aim to have your materials look like products (brochures, post cards, posters); be careful to consider perceived 'spend' if externally produced; try to achieve polished materials with in-house resources. This consideration is generally more of a concern in government and not-for-profit environments.

Commitment – Impacted stakeholders will always want to know 'what is changing' if this detail is unavailable, they will want to know 'when will I know'. Similar to the dialogue on timelines and dates in the previous chapter, be careful here on commitments you make that may not be within your span of control – do not provide commitments you cannot, or are unlikely to make. You will be held to any commitments you make, including dates you specify to provide materials by. Provide indicative timelines until more details are firmed up. You will lose a lot of confidence and trust if you communicate dates that are then missed. If you make a commitment, follow through; always provide what you can, even if it is not the full detail. Often, communicating the process to get to the point where the detail will be known can alleviate concerns. There are of course, many examples of where we have all communicated dates that have been missed and the response from staff is manageable. The theme in this chapter is to 'avoid' eroding staff trust as much as possible as this will lead to better overall adoption and change outcomes.

At the commencement of a change program it can be helpful to communicate that there are two approaches to managing change:

1. Everything is decided behind closed doors and staff are advised just prior to the changes being implemented. (not recommended) *OR*
2. Staff are advised from the start, so that they may be part of the process and contribute to shaping the change.

Most people will indicate a preference for Option 2. However, making this point is mostly to iterate why the full detail is unknown and to encourage participation. This message should be followed by a range of ways for staff to engage in the change.

13

The Change Armour

Recent trends in change management have been to standardise templates, so that consultants aren't brought in each time a change is implemented to develop bespoke tools for the same activities.

There are a number of online packages now available to support the adoption of change. This trend has assisted to develop a foundational change management capability in many organisations; however, it provides only the very basics for managing change.

At any rate, these tools are beneficial for incremental changes, but largely don't provide for the human responses to an organisation that is transforming. This leads us to the concept of change resilience and the reality that your value is more who you are and not what you do.

Change leaders tend to be a particular breed of people who naturally gravitate to 'soft skills' and personal development. That is not to say that these skills cannot be developed.

It may require more attention to these areas to successfully lead and facilitate change if 'soft skills' are not the preferred way of working, this is particularly prevalent in Financial Services organisations where many leaders commence their careers in roles with strong analytical, financial and technical capabilities and have a greater need to develop soft skills as their career progresses.

The creation of a change capable organisation focuses predominantly on the development of soft skills to create a network of 'change focused' employees. The intention is that these new ways of responding to emotional situations become more prevalent in the organisation.

Case in point: an organisation with a 'culture of respect' experienced a rumbling of negativity towards a new organisational structure. The negativity was not to how the organisation was structured, but to who was appointed to various positions. The corridor conversations were lacking respect, managers and change agents were able to identify and report what was happening, however hadn't been upskilled sufficiently to be able to respond confidently and effectively to the negativity.

The following section introduces a concept for considering all the various 'soft skills' that can assist us to become more change resilient. It was born from a conversation with a fellow change professional where we were considering the difference between managing people's responses to change as a 'change manager' compared to managing peoples responses to change as an operational line manager. The line manager is largely more invested in the individuals, due to professional working relationships, that in many instances have spanned years or decades. The line manager however, has an operational focus and has to 'switch hats' to focus on themselves in a way that creates a space to support others and their various responses to change.

The idea of the 'change armour' emerged as a concept that demonstrates how we need to separate ourselves from others' responses. It is a way of being aware of what is going on for us and to build our resilience so that we can better lead and support others.

The change armour is built with all the skills that a change manager wears all of the time versus the skills that an operational manager wears 'some of the time'. The idea considers the merits of wearing this skill set full- or part time.

At any rate it can be emotionally draining to be 'wearing any skill set' full time if it does not come naturally to you. Applying the skills becomes more manageable if you can build an awareness of what the skills are, how they are applied, when they are most useful and your own physical response to maintain these states for long periods of time.

As a verb, armour is to provide (someone) with emotional, social, or other defences. In this section we detail all the aspects of the 'armour' that are applicable and beneficial for those leading change.

A change program should never be seen as entering into battle. It is even helpful to think that 'if you prepare yourself for a battle, you will find yourself in a war'.

Rather the idea of the change armour is about protection. Protection of self. A delineation between what is 'yours', and what belongs to someone else. Emotionally.

One of my most commonly used coaching phrases is 'not about you', to remind people when they are investing their emotions and energy in someone else's journey. So often we drain our energy and attention mulling over a situation or response from someone that is very much prompted by their own experiences.

Identifying when something is about your own actions and not theirs and vice versa can be a liberating and renewing technique. If you can separate your actions as a 'change leader' from the responses of those impacted in a period of change (or responding to life in general), you will develop a reliable set of skills to navigate the emotional aspects of the human experience.

The change armour throughout the next section focuses on a 'whole of body' approach. Each element of the armour represents a physical and emotional awareness of self and from this awareness, ways to self-adjust actions and responses. The more the armour is explored, the more it is strengthened and developed, providing a strong foundation for the most challenging transformations.

HELMET

Thoughts, judgments, your own ladder of inference, avoiding assumptions.

- Be aware of your thoughts and what has prompted them; is it your own past experiences with change?
- Be aware of all elements of your 'ladder of inference'. Perhaps there are previous experiences in your employment that have added to your 'pool of data'.
- There are no right or wrong responses to change. Everyone experiences their own journey in their own time; be mindful that you are not making judgments about other people's responses based on your views and expectations.
- Avoid assumptions about people and their wants, needs and aspirations; as a prompt think of the Jo-Hari window (a framework for exploring known knowns and unknowns in yourself and others developed by Joseph Luft and Harrington Ingham in 1955). It is a good frame to view what you may not be aware of about an individual.
- Create a space to think. Remove distractions and allow yourself time to contemplate, to mull over, to reconsider.
- Allow yourself time to be inspired. Find sources of inspiration and apply them to utilise their value in planning and strategy sessions.
- Brain power: devise strategies that capitalise on the brain power of others, create complex questions and problems that source insightful consideration from stakeholders.
- Run problem solving competitions that look for innovative solutions from stakeholders.

FACE GUARD

Your communications filter; choose your words wisely, focus on language.

- We communicate with our whole bodies, but we primarily communicate with our words and our expressions. Our whole face, including where our eyes focus, the muscles – including frowning and smiling – all tell a story, are you aware of what your expressions communicate to others?
- Be mindful of what you are 'not saying', people in transition will often assume the worst, ensure you are clearly balancing the 'what it is' with 'what it is not'.
- Carefully selected language can reinforce your message. For example: 'are there any questions?' Will receive a different response to 'are there any thoughts, comments, views, questions, suggestions?'
- Exploring language can align a group of disparate views, a dictionary and thesaurus should be used frequently, discuss what the words mean to you and solicit views on what terms mean to others, it is often not the final word that you choose that is most important; it is the conversation that you've had to ensure everyone is on the same page and understands what is meant.
- Your vocal tone will convey an array of meanings to those with whom you are communicating. Are you aware of what your voice says about you? A rushed pace can convey dismissiveness; a higher pitch can convey incredulousness. A music theatre director shared a useful idea, that 'nerves show an audition panel respect'. This concept assists to 'own' and overcome fears of a nervous voice, but more particularly to be aware of the full spectrum of responses that may be gleaned from vocal 'tone'.

SHOULDER GUARDS

A symbol of standing tall, reframing, finding positivity and different ways to problem solve.

- Be aware of the difference your posture can make to how you feel. Raising and releasing your shoulders and aligning your physique can be a powerful way to re-set when confronting a difficult situation.
- Reframe a situation with your body, your words, your thoughts, your outlook, and your stance.
- Be confident in your decisions, your approach, your own truth… Be full of trust.
- Positivity and negativity are infectious, choose how you want to feel about a situation and work towards 'living it in action'.
- Be courageous in the actions you take and finding new ways to look at problems and solve them.
- Be aware of 'carrying the weight of the world', share the load, so that there is ownership and collaboration amongst the stakeholder groups.
- Think outside the box, 'shift your stance' be creative and challenge the status quo and 'the way we've always done things', what if…?

BODY PLATE

Empathy, be guided by your instincts and intuition, follow your gut

- 'Dis-ease', finding things 'difficult to digest', wearing your 'heart on your sleeve' are all sayings inspired by the core of our body. They relate to how our feelings affect our state of being.
- Use your sense of 'knowing'; sometimes it's hard to pinpoint what causes our sense of what feels right in a situation, trust in your previous learnings to guide positive ways to move through situations.
- Undertake regular 'pulse-checks', which include finding multiple sources of information and inputs to inform your sense of how things are progressing.
- Be present in the moment with how you are feeling, so as not to impose your emotions into someone else's situation.
- Be aware of where in your body you are holding or carrying stresses. Focusing on them, exploring them in detail, rather than just being 'aware' of them, will help to shift and alleviate any tensions.
- Avoid 'bottling' things up, the cork is known to pop under the stress of a challenging change program.
- 'I've got your back', support others to be successful by providing encouragement to be courageous, and work in new ways.
- Flush out that which is no longer required. Start workshops with activities that assist people to leave behind previous experiences and frustrations.

ELBOW SHIELD

Your connectors, build strong relationships and prioritise engagement

- Consider appropriate times to reach out and to connect with others, this could be with peers, mentors, networks and team members.
- Think of 'the olive branch' where you may have had difficult relationships. An offer of reconciliation is the 'restoration of relations'.
- Connect others. You may have strong relationships already in place, but what about others? Can you facilitate an introduction, or are you aware of similar interests that others may have?
- Use the Jo-Hari window here as inspiration, what are the unknowns that your connectors could uncover?
- Un-cross your arms. Be 'open' to new relationships, experiences and learnings.
- Embrace the change, try to 'wrap your arms around it' be clear on scope and focus on inclusiveness.

HAND PLATES

The touch points to get things done, get busy creating, suggesting, writing, re-doing, re-shaping, producing.

- 'Many hands make light work – use them.'
- Contribute by creating interesting content. This could be words, visuals, stories, Case Studies, videos, cartoons, anecdotes, quotes.
- Translate messages to your team… make the change relevant by detailing what the change will look like for impacted staff.
- Capture questions, do not be afraid of not knowing the answer, sometimes the most helpful response is providing a more detailed set of questions that need to be answered.
- Count to ten … Create lists: check lists, to-do lists, shopping lists, wish lists, action lists, contributor lists, awards lists, contact lists, Top 10 lists. There is nothing more rewarding than the feeling of completion.
- Use creativity to engage in new ways of working, make it fun to get involved, use colour, be tactile, find interactive ways to engage.
- Hold an art exhibition to demonstrate different ways of interpreting, creating, presenting what is aiming to be achieved. Such as for your value chain, or operating environment.

LEGS

Maintain momentum, default to forward, keep moving, don't stop, don't wait.

- Moving forward will maintain momentum, demonstrating what you are doing and achieving will inspire others to do the same. 'Default to Forward': if one pathway is paused, or blocked, walk another path until they meet up again.

- Keep energy and engagement levels up by having new ways to be involved in the process of change, physically get people moving, to a new location for meetings, meet in the park, or have a walking group that discusses 'hot topics' related to the project.

- When you feel, or hear 'I'm waiting for...' re-cap what you do know, new questions may arise, that help to 'kick-start' a new wave of activities.

- Show the journey walked to date, continually demonstrate the path that has already been completed, it will re-align and re-engage, and build confidence through a sense of achievement.

- Create 'choose your own adventure' materials that demonstrate how future changes may play out in different scenarios and with different audience groups.

- Do a floor walk to understand what others are experiencing, think of this as an interactive survey.

- 'Walk in my shoes' job swap, or job shadow to understand what others are experiencing.

- See the legs as providing stability, where required; stand still, take stock, and decide which path to walk next.

SWORD AND SHIELD

Use tools and balance to arm yourself: A sword to cut through to core issues, balanced with a shield to protect integrity and core values.

- 'Arm yourself' with information, be seen as a source of the most up to date materials and key messages, be a trusted ally.
- Focus on what matters; distil information to the top 3 or 5 key pieces of information, provide executive summaries.
- Be targeted in your messaging, provide different levels of information for those with different levels of interest.
- Use 'need to know' as your guide. What does your audience need to know at each point in the change? What information is critical to their operations?
- Use prioritisation planning to chunk down the change to make the transition manageable, look at the tasks that have a high level of benefit/positive impact and cross reference on a matrix with the tasks that involve a high level of effort /resourcing/ dependencies. Use this effort/impact matrix to align all stakeholders on focus areas.
- Slice and dice, chunk down the activities into manageable work packages. Stage gate your activities to achieve wins sooner.
- Create tools and templates that standardise, align and focus attention.
- 'Divide and conquer' celebrate successes and acknowledge all the contributions, the parts that have come together collaboratively to achieve success as a whole.

14

Responses to Change

At around the nine-month (or 3/4s of the way) point in a change and more particularly a transformation program, you get something that I affectionately call the 'bounce back' phenomenon. This is the point where the reality versus expectations paradigm kicks in.

You've spent a significant period of time building trust and empowering and encouraging individuals to align to the vision, get involved and contribute to make it happen. As a change leader, you've set the goal at the extreme. You have a vision and you've been talking the talk, walking the walk and walking the talk. As go-live approaches, stakeholders start to see the shifts occurring across the organisation, but there is a disconnect between where they are, where they want to be, and where they can be … and it really starts to show; you can 'feel' it.

This sense of disconnect will cause unease, confusion, instability, drop in performance, drop in engagement and a lack of trust in the vision, the program, the approach and the benefits. It will feel like your program is unravelling … This is where the true change capacity of your organisation will show. This is the environment in which the greatest change occurs.

In this void, in the centre of the performance dip, or change curve, there is a lull which is experienced differently by everyone. Individuals will fill the void with a response best suited to them. This default response is their resilience and is a coping mechanism to 'self-manage' through the period of uncertainty. There is no right or wrong response here; all are valid responses to change.

Understanding some of the common responses will assist an organisation to identify if they have a good cross section of engagement, or if everyone is responding in a similar way, you may need to understand what is being experienced and why.

Use these following categories as a guide in conjunction with applying the Transformation[3] understanding of how things transform. You may find that the organisation as a whole are in the 'sweet spot' of the model with all three elements in balance. However, as an example, at an individual level someone may have invested too heavily in the 'Destination' element and may need to be re-balanced by focusing their 'Awareness' in all the things they've achieved to date.

Exploring where individuals are at in the 'bounce back' stages of a change program assists in building your Awareness element, providing guidance by helping people understand why they are experiencing what they are experiencing. If you find, for instance, that you have no 'opportunists' you may want to include in your destination 'creating a space where opportunists can flourish'.

A summary and dialogue of some of the groups and categories of responses you may witness are as follows:

GOING BACK
A return to what we've always done – a better the devil you know scenario.

BLAME
Why isn't someone else filling the void for me?

WAITING
Like a tortoise, the head, legs and arms retreat, the thinking, moving, doing stops.

OPPORTUNISTS
Suggestions, proactive, find another way, take a chance, initiate.

LEADERS
Re-group, re-adjust, re-affirm, re-boot, re-assure, re-align.

All of these responses (and many unique variations) are needed through a period of change; if the whole organisation were in one category or another, successful change would not occur.

The people that tend to 'go-back' provide your foundation, they tend to 'go-back' to the things that they know work. For many individuals, this response provides stability and a way of contributing value in periods of uncertainty. They help to manage your risk and ensure that you don't 'throw the baby out with the bath water'. If the whole organisation, or a significant part of the organisation, find themselves in the 'go-back' category, you'll find that you simply don't change at all.

The 'blame' group want to be on board; they're aligned to the vision, but they are lacking some confidence (trust) in the program. They need to see it working, yet they feel like they have needs that aren't being met. This group are actually on board but are looking outside of themselves for the change to occur. The blame group are powerful at this point in the program for two reasons: they trigger the opportunists and leaders into action and when you get the blame group to look inwards (take ownership) they become opportunists and leaders. Those responding in this way tend to be quite vocal, which makes a change leaders job easy if you listen to what they are asking for! (Apply T3 thinking here to move them from being too much in the 'Guidance' element, to re-balancing with 'Awareness' and 'Destination' activities at an individual level.)

The 'waiters' keep you alive through periods of change; they often will focus on BAU, provide stability, they won't be detractors, or noisy through periods of uncertainty, but they will self-manage by retreating. You may find your early adopters disappear from your forums, have a quiet word with you about how they're feeling, or why they are where they are. They are re-grouping within themselves and will respond well to your encouragement to 'self-care'. You may sense a vibe of disappointment as they re-adjust their expectations to their present reality. Reassure them that this is a perfectly valid response to change. They are in the sweet spot of how things transform but are not presently 'taking action'. Joining them together with an opportunist may make a powerful cross organisational partnership.

Your 'opportunists' will want to fill the void; they see an opportunity and they strike, they are your entrepreneurs, your future leaders, they will keep propelling your program forward, they will capture your Success Stories and demonstrate to those 'going back', in the 'blame group' or the 'waiters' that they can trust in the program, it is changing the organisation, and it is delivering success.

If there are too many opportunists, you can find yourself being pulled in too many directions, there will be 'too-much' going on, people will be stressed, at capacity and overwhelmed. Leaders can find opportunists challenging, but opportunists essentially need leaders to keep them focused, on track and to help be leaders of their initiatives in the organisation (see chapter 16 on empowerment).

The 'leaders' are pivotal. If you don't have leaders stepping in to re-group, re-adjust, re-affirm, re-boot, re-assure, or re-align, the opportunists will be seen as the default leaders and the negative symptoms of too many opportunists will be the prevailing sentiment in your organisation. Your leaders won't necessarily be the most senior people in your organisation. Leaders are those who align to the Vision, see what is and isn't working, and keep leading the way towards the destination. The leaders both respond to the 'push' to change and maintain momentum by 'pulling' (inspiring, motivating, role modelling) individuals forward.

If everybody in an organisation is 'leading', there may be a risk that not enough focus on your foundations and BAU is occurring.

Most of the attention in a change program goes into ways to encourage and support people to be opportunists and leaders. This ensures that the program has good ownership and doesn't stagnate. What is required is a balanced approach, that acknowledges that all responses to change are valid, and required, to ensure successful change in your organisation.

15

When the Ground Beneath You Shifts

After significant effort in planning, transitioning, assessing, responding, managing behaviours, and responses to change, you start to feel the shift occurring in the organisation. You are edging towards the tipping point (where the majority of people are moving to the changed state). As individuals shift from the responses you see in the 'bounce back' stage into working in the new ways, there are a range of new experiences that you will observe.

Again, they will be different for everyone, and they will occur at different times. At this point in the program you will have people at the full range of points along the change curve, so whilst you are supporting some individuals in their final stage of transitioning, you will also still be supporting individuals who will say, 'I'm not sure what the program is aiming to achieve?' even with the very best communications plan having been rolled out!

This chapter provides a range of supplementary tools and techniques for understanding and responding to individuals at all points along the change journey. It is aimed at providing 'New Perspectives' (Guidance) to help shift people from where they are (Awareness) to where you want them to be (Destination). Remember how infectious positivity is, perhaps applying these techniques to one individual who is stuck will make a significant change across your whole organisation, particularly if it is an executive or senior leader who has been resistant or undermining of your transformation efforts.

WALK IN MY SHOES
Ask yourself: 'If I am impacted by this change, what will my responses be?'

We understand through Maslow's hierarchy of needs that there is a strong need for individuals to feel safety, to feel that there will not be loss. Our sense of safety and the interests that we are keen to protect vary considerably from person to person, so endeavour to walk in someone else's shoes and explore what their interests are.

Equality is another core need of individuals, if it seems that someone has been privy to information, or opportunities that have not been available equally across the organisation, we can become disillusioned with the process.

When providing opportunities to engage, or to express interest in being involved for impacted stakeholders, try not to limit the audience unless there is a valid and reasonable reason to do so. Play out various scenarios, for different stakeholders, walk in their shoes and assess whether individuals may feel excluded.

We have needs to be included, to be provided with the opportunity to understand, to be informed of the rationale, and to be able to discern for ourselves, how we can best contribute our unique value to the initiatives.

We have a need to trust in others. To know that when a commitment is made it will be adhered to. Continue to walk in others shoes throughout the change by asking questions and genuinely being interested in others motivations and needs.

EMBRACING AMBIGUITY
Embracing ambiguity is one of the fundamentals in affecting change. Resilience can be described as the ability to maintain oneself at our optimum state through periods of uncertainty.

The periods of uncertainty vary significantly dependent on the type of change being implemented. However, at the transformational end of the spectrum, where multiple aspects are changing, there will be ambiguity.

Many times, stakeholders will say, 'Just tell me what I need to do differently when you know.' In transactional and operational roles there will be many people who are happy to respond to the changes in this way. This is exactly what you need, as these are the individuals that provide your stability. However, there will be others in these teams that are leaders and influencers that may already have different ideas for improvements, if you just 'tell them what to do differently', they may not be so eager to comply. It is for these people that change programs are inclusive and collaborative, so that we can source their ideas and utilise their knowledge as a Subject Matter Expert (SME) and assist them in aligning and implementing changes that will support the organisation to get where it needs to be.

Periods of ambiguity also provide opportunities to create the desired culture. Focusing on spans of control and spans of influence will help navigate through the periods of uncertainty. Together with all the core change capabilities around inspiring, motivating and empowering individuals to shape the change which ultimately minimises the ambiguity experienced.

A final thought on ambiguity: aiming for the 'path of least resistance' may not affect your change outcomes positively, you may find for example, that there is a lack of engagement behind the lack of resistance. Aim for inspiring stakeholders to have passion and purpose.

STATING THE BLEEDING OBVIOUS

Sometimes it is the simplest and easiest things that are overlooked when they are most likely to make the biggest impact.

Over time, culture in organisations set the new norm, and it is often the little things that are first to go when there are competing priorities and staff are under the pump. But it is the simple things that will most likely improve an organisations ability to successfully implement change.

These simplest of things satisfy our hierarchy of needs. They help shift us forward, brighten our day, assist us to reconnect and deal with periods of uncertainty.

What are these simplest things that make such a difference?

- Smile.
- Thank you (even for the most left-field suggestions).
- Hold a door, offer to help, acknowledge workload, ask about interests, show compassion, make a cuppa, tidy up for someone, review a document, offer a chat.
- Thank you (providing acknowledgement, being valued).
- Smile (creating a space, being supportive).

Ever felt that you have been considered as patronising when facilitating a conversation around change and engagement? It is an easy thing to do, because often you can find yourself stating the bleeding obvious. But sometimes it just must be done, we need the constant reminders, the persistence, to be re-energised as leaders. Particularly after months of trying to cut through repeating messages.

If you find that you are presenting on change or engagement and you receive a lacklustre response from your audience, it is likely to be because your audience is thinking:

'I can't believe those simple things just hadn't occurred to me!'

AWAKENING HEARTS AND MINDS

Somewhere, someone set an expectation that change management is about 'winning the hearts and minds'. If this is the premise of a change program, it is likely that this sentiment will create the wrong culture for the change you are trying to achieve.

The very definition of the word 'winning' is counter-intuitive to the premise of people needing to be part of the process of change to ensure its success.

Winning is defined as: gaining, resulting in, or relating to victory in a contest, or competition. Winning is not about facilitating, collaborating, innovating, empowerment, accountability. It is the very opposite.

The hearts and minds, however, is what you want people to bring to the table in a change program, hearts bringing compassion, empathy, truth and passion, bringing smarter, clever, new, creative, innovative approaches.

Your very definition of success in leading change is your ability to 'awaken' to inspire, to empower, to support, to nurture, to facilitate the very best that your stakeholders have to offer.

If you feel as though there is something to be won, by its very definition you have already lost.

Similar to empowerment, which we will explore in the next chapter, some senior managers feel that awakening hearts and minds can 'stir the beast'. This will only be the case if you are making assumptions and judgements on the value of another individual's passion, ideas and intellect.

Awakening hearts and minds is a process of facilitating and nurturing the contributions that are made towards the shared destination. Like any other skill it will often take time and energy to develop.

Awakening hearts and minds is less about being inspirational and more about leveraging your skills to 'create a space' for the awakening to occur. Other change skills outlined in this book including 'relinquishing any personal need for validation' are also fundamental at this time.

Quite often, individuals carry the experiences of the past and previous change programs for a very long time. I have had stakeholders quote changes to me that occurred for them over a decade previously. After a damaging experience, it can take significantly longer for a new sense of 'trust' to be established.

It's not that individuals can't, or don't want to be inspired, and contribute ideas and make things better – it's more often than not that someone has shot them down or dismissed their ideas in the past, making it difficult for them to trust in the engagement process again.

The persistence required in these situations from your change leadership is not something that can be measured. It is required in every interaction, at the start and end of every meeting, be unwavering in facilitating a space where individuals are supported, encouraged, nurtured to contribute. (Note: this excludes supporting behaviours that are outside the values of the organisation, which should be addressed through existing management practices and policies).

A helpful formula for awakening hearts and minds is:

Set the vision + Create a space – Your own stuff x Lots of time = Passion and Purpose

TOP DOWN, BOTTOM UP, AND SPANS OF CONTROL

After many months of asking stakeholders to contribute, to engage and to help 'shape the change', you reach that point where expectations and reality collide. For managers in particular, spans of control and their influencing environment will play a role in how successfully they will be able to drive the change forward in their area.

Managers will feel a combination of:

- the things they are being expected to do by their manager
- the things they are expecting of their manager
- the things they are expecting of their staff
- the things their staff are expecting of them.

All four of these influencing factors are important to keep the transition moving forward. Managers may have had expectations of the change that haven't been met, and can often disengage, which results in a loss of momentum. It is important to focus on the span of control that they have for the change, and to re-empower, to focus on what they can change within their influencing environment.

It is helpful to also talk with stakeholders about 'degrees of change'. How far along the spectrum have we progressed, and how much further can we go? Reflect on how we have achieved the changes that have been made to date, has it all been top down, or have some initiatives been driven bottom up to meet the vision? Has there been good engagement and collaboration between executive, managers and staff?

A change that is all 'push' from the bottom up, will likely result in many different initiatives that are not aligned to a shared vision and destination. The initiatives will likely not have management support, will be duplicated effort and not realise a defined set of benefits.

Conversely, a change that is all 'pull' from the top will be slow, hard, and likely ineffective, as staff won't have had the opportunity to contribute. They won't have ownership and the ability to ask for the things they require to engage in and adopt the changes.

If a manager is feeling that the expectations on them are out of balance with what they are expecting from others (either up, down or vertically across their peer group), it is worth reflecting on the push/pull paradigm within their span of control, to re-focus on moving the change forward.

Where you find that there is a break in the communications and expectations; either up, down or across, there will likely be symptoms; feeling stuck, overwhelmed, disconnected. From a simple conversation, you will be able to discern from these symptoms why the transformation has lost traction for them. Overlay the Transformation[3] elements ... review and respond.

Tip: avoid asking questions such as: 'How are feeling about the change?' Whilst this is a good question you will likely elicit 'good' as a compliant response.

Rather, ask a thought-provoking question which you can dive deeper into and really understand what's going on for the stakeholder. Some suggestions:

- What are you most excited about achieving as part of this change?
- What's the one thing in the transformation that will make your job easier?
- How have you found supporting your team through the uncertainty?
- What change skills have you picked up from your peer group?
- What role can you see yourself performing in the future?

16

Empowerment

The problem of empowerment in the corporate world is arguably not a problem at all but scratch the surface of this buzzword and many an executive run in fear. The modern office carries many a term that is misunderstood and/or not put into practice for the benefit of both individuals and organisations. It is a leading reason that change, transformation, and culture building activities fail to deliver the desired results.

WHAT IS EMPOWERMENT?
Empowerment is defined as giving someone the power or authority to do something. A 'Culture of Empowerment' is often used by organisations undertaking transformations to encourage staff to think smarter, work with innovation and to take accountability.

WHAT DOES EMPOWERMENT IN THE WORKPLACE LOOK LIKE?

Many organisations constrict staff position descriptions to the point that they are crippling to an individual's ability to contribute. According to Maslow's hierarchy of needs, the 'self-actualising' part of our selves is oftentimes unmet in the workplace.

We know that many people require structure and security – which satisfies other traits on the hierarchy of needs – but not at the detriment of being a contributor. Over time, with enough reinforcement of 'only delivering against a position description' individuals believe their worth is nothing outside of this and disempowerment kicks in.

HOW DOES EMPOWERING EMPLOYEES BENEFIT ORGANISATIONS?

Empowered employees deliver their greatest value, empowered employees will align to, and deliver against the vision because doing so enables them to feel more empowered. Empowered individuals will go above and beyond with individual commitments to continuously improve, contribute, shape, create, drive and grow your organisation.

Empowered individuals drive greater capabilities in managers and leaders to find ways to nurture, mentor, support, drive and guide the empowered individual to success (see next section – Why Leaders Fear Empowerment).

Empowered employees will surprise you. They will deliver innovation that is truly the inspiration that you were looking for (as opposed to the 'innovation' that is just doing what we've always done, but a little different).

Empowered employees will be inspirational, when they find their rhythm and 'flow' you will find their ideas flourish and they will inspire others to be in their flow also.

Empowered employees are resilient, they know how to self-manage, to re-group, to find another way, to learn to grow, to challenge to succeed.

WHY LEADERS FEAR EMPOWERMENT

Empowered individuals drive greater capabilities in managers and leaders, prompting them to find ways to nurture, mentor, support, drive and guide the empowered individual to success. This is exactly why leaders fear empowerment: it forces leadership capabilities to be greater than those that they have empowered.

Leaders fear 'rogue, empowered individuals' because there can be a perception that they are difficult to manage. If you have 'rogue empowered individuals' it is because you haven't clearly, repeatedly, tiresomely and effectively communicated and engaged your staff in your vision and the desired destination.

The poorer the engagement, the more problematic untamed empowerment may become. If staff are disengaged and not aligned to the organisation's vision and objectives, an empowerment drive won't help your cause. It will result in those rogue operators, the 'opportunists' who will take their new empowerment eagerly, but they won't have the right direction to focus their empowered selves towards.

Leaders have a tendency to 'manage' who they empower, which begins a cyclic reinforcement of disempowerment for those that are not deemed the right candidates. It can be a powerful technique to invest more time to shape positive empowerment in staff who would other times not be selected for development opportunities.

Consider a tightly controlled environment that is driven by process and KPIs. This workplace will likely disempower individuals to a point where staff relinquish their empowerment and a lack of staff engagement soon follows.

TECHNIQUES FOR POSITIVE EMPOWERMENT

In the context of a clearly defined Vision, empower away. Define what empowerment looks like, then explain why it is desired and what benefits there are for both the individual and the organisation.

Make a commitment. What will your leadership team do to support those staff stepping into the empowerment zone? How will you create a safe and supportive environment for any fears of failure?

Explore concepts of the holistic being; bring in speakers to talk on inspirational topics. Encourage wellness, awareness, personal development, coaching and mentoring.

Capture Case Studies from other organisations and your own that demonstrate positive empowerment.

Establish an empowerment network, to support, drive and inspire empowerment in your organisation.

Empower your staff to devise ways to support their own empowerment!

17

Change in Leadership

Stakeholder question: 'What do I do if the current CEO doesn't re-sign for another contract? It will only be twelve months into the changed environment. I'm worried that someone new will come in and take us in a different direction.'

It would be fair to say that a change in leadership scenario typically occurs 'pre-conception' of a change program. It is rare that external change support would already be in place to assist with this type of transition. Specialist change management advice is generally brought in after the decision to change. However, as the Transformation³ methodology details, the change will be more successful the sooner you consider how to approach the change and begin to balance the elements early.

The 'change in leadership' change, in itself, provides a valid reason for seeking change guidance, prior to determining what form of changes the new leader wants to introduce. When commencing in a new position, most leaders will take one of two courses of action, influenced be a vast array of contextual scenarios:

a) embark on a period of observation prior to setting a new course

b) enter with a bang, launching a number of new initiatives off the bat

HOW PEOPLE RESPOND TO NEW LEADERS
The commencement of new leadership generally prompts the following responses and behaviours from staff:

- Waiting, sitting on the fence, undecided on sense of loyalty
- Grief, sense that good work under previous leadership will be lost, discontinued
- Excitement, hope of improvement, new world, high expectations

The Transformation[3] elements are already at play. If people are in the waiting space, it is likely that they are focused heavily in the 'Awareness' element, but the destination has not been clearly articulated. Individuals or organisations heavily in the 'Awareness' element can stagnate, getting caught in a cyclical loop of doing things as we've always done, without the 'Destination' element, they can also 'go back' to a time of more security, comfort, stability.

If people experience an element of grief, it is likely that they have been 'shocked into a destination'. Too heavy a focus on the 'Destination' element, can leave people overwhelmed. The new vision is so far removed from where people are that it feels like it cannot be achieved, the destination if communicated in new language and style can feel foreign. If it feels foreign it may not acknowledge the 'heritage' of the organisation that people are attached too.

There is a common reflection in change theory that people need to be 'pushed off the cliff' (metaphorically of course) into the change curve (or chasm of ambiguity). It can be important to do so, but it is important also to secure a rope first (one that can be detached once the other side of the cavern has been reached). The 'rope' in this instance is the continuation of what has worked well in the past; the acknowledgement of effort and contribution, of individuals' personal blood, sweat and tears. It is balancing out the 'Destination' element with a healthy sense of 'Awareness'. The 'Guidance' element can be stabilising in this process too, with a focus on confidence building and demonstration of 'how we will get there', which could include frameworks, strategies and methodologies that are accepted and trusted by the organisation. For a new leader to share stories of how they have achieved similar destinations in other organisations would be an appropriate 'Guidance' activity.

Excitement, hope, new world, and expectations all sound like a brilliant place for your staff to be upon your commencement in a new leadership position. You have clearly articulated your desired destination and you have spent significant focus on acknowledging the current state and building awareness. However, this is not a place to linger for too long. The activities you undertake as a new leader to acknowledge the past and set the course for the future could likely cause your employees to find themselves too much in the Guidance Element, as in, someone else is going to make their world better for them. This is a tricky balance for new leaders to ensure that in setting the direction that staff have been included in shaping what that will look like.

We could divert at this point to an in-depth dialogue on leadership styles, but this will likely be another book. The Transformation³ methodology requires particular leadership attributes and the application and adjustment of personal style to facilitate and support the approach. Most leaders are adept at identifying their personal leadership style and are encouraged to identify from the tools and techniques throughout this book where gaps in personal leadership style may be problematic in leading a transformation. The application of Transformation³ for personal growth (chapter 21) provides a roadmap for this activity where required.

HOW TO MANAGE PEOPLE'S RESPONSES TO NEW LEADERS

The following section should be considered in the context of the 'push/pull' paradigm (chapter 15), which is essentially the balance of a top down/bottom up change environment.

The pre-conception phase of a change program can be managed smoothly and effectively with a focus on the objectives of different stakeholder groups. If we look at the objectives of staff within an organisation and the new leader themselves, they are likely aligned. For example:

- Staff want their previous work and contribution to be acknowledged and to continue doing the things that work well. New leaders want to understand the great things that have occurred in an organisation and to ensure, for the bottom line, that they continue.

- Staff want to deliver their highest value and to work where they can have pride in what they do. Leaders want people to work to their greatest capacity, delivering value and being proud of their organisation's contribution.
- Staff want to contribute their ideas and suggestions for improvement having them considered by those that they look up to. Leaders want staff to come up with ways to do things better, they are after all the experts in their job (review the empowerment dialogue, chapter 16)
- Staff will want to know what, how, why and when it's changing so that they can get on board and can/will change. New leaders want staff to adopt their changes. (If you're currently in the midst of a change, consider this bullet a checkpoint: Do you know what is changing, why it's changing, how it's changing and when it's changing?)

This alignment of objectives should effectively act as goal posts, when commencing in a new leadership position. Some suggested activities include:

- Encourage staff to capture and submit 'values stories', i.e. a time where I have contributed the greatest value to the organisation, my team, our stakeholders.
- Run SWOT analysis type sessions. Some existing leaders will feel uncomfortable with this activity

as it implies that they don't already know this information. A simple reframe can assist: 'I feel I have a strong understanding of the existing successes and opportunities of the organisation, but I am also keen to hear from staff to ensure that the thinking is aligned and to ensure that I test and validate any assumptions I may have made prior to working through where we should direct our attention.'

- Implement culture initiatives. Define the aspect of the culture you want to have, for example: empowerment, innovation and contribution, and establish channels for staff to input their ideas. The following points provide a helpful formula for response:

  Thank you for speaking up and contributing + we appreciate the suggestion + (one of the following three responses):

  - It's a great idea, is aligned to our vision, and will be implemented
  - The idea shows thoughtful consideration; however, it is not aligned to the current vision (+ why)
  - It's a great idea, is aligned to our Vision, but we don't think it is achievable just yet, we will include this in our future plans (maintain a visible log for staff to follow)

- Establish a solid project management approach that is aligned to expectations across the organisation, is communicated to build confidence and clearly treats the who, what, why, when how, of each aspect of the change.

A change in leadership is a change in and of itself. It is a change, by its very nature, that is 'done to' staff, but it doesn't have to feel this way. A solid six months of activities to 'manage the change' of a new leader's commencement will set up the organisation for any initiative that the new leader wishes to implement. Staff will be 'ready to change', engaged, aligned, and supportive of your vision before you have even determined what it is you want to achieve.

Reset Strategy #8

Apply the Transformation Model to an aspect of your leadership you would like to transform.

Guidance Element

18

Getting it Right

Doing the right things, at the right time, with the right people, in the right way is important. Seems simple right?

RIGHT THINGS
Why it's important ...

The concept of the 'right things' is fairly self-explanatory, it's about choosing wisely, being considered, experienced and confident that the path ahead and the activities will deliver the right result. But you can't always get a good idea of the 'right things' from a text book or what has worked somewhere else previously.

Every situation and individual is different and quite often in a change program a project manager will work tirelessly to a schedule or game plan that receives no traction. The tasks may be completed – albeit slowly, and without much enthusiasm – but there will be no ownership in the business and it will most likely fail in its implementation.

Hopefully the concept of 'balancing the elements' shared throughout this book has highlighted the need to 'assess' what is going on in your organisation first and appropriately choosing the right activities to ensure you stay in the 'sweet spot' where things transform.

How it fails ...

Not doing the right things is evident with hindsight, but oftentimes the path taken was the only available path at the time. Leaders must ask themselves: *Was this the right path at the time?* How can we improve upon this path to ensure that it will be as successful as possible now and in the future?

As an example, assigning accountabilities early in a program of work is 9 times out of 10 the 'right thing' to be doing. However, often there is a cultural hurdle to individuals taking this level of responsibility. Pushing the issue will cause resistance and disengagement. The 'right thing' in this scenario then becomes a suite of alternative ways of ensuring accountability is taken.

Change leadership is the ability to be creative to 'influence' the activities towards what needs to be done. In this instance it might be a focus on educating, building confidence, identifying and strengthening the case for change, all of which are in aid of and support for the original activity required to assign accountability.

Why it fails ...

Making assumptions. Assuming how individuals will or should respond is the primary way that activities fail in change programs. Failing to consider how different individuals will respond to activities causes a disconnect that will ultimately impede your success.

While on the surface, the planned activity may seem to be the 'right thing' in the methodology, or project management experience, it may not always be the case once presented to stakeholders. Scratch the surface and probe to find the source of stakeholder resistance, or lack of traction. A different set of primary activities may be required first, which will enable the planned activities to become the 'right activities' at the 'right time'.

RIGHT TIME
Why it's important ...

Project scheduling to identify critical pathways in complex project implementations is a well-know and adopted step in all change programs. However, in this context the 'right time' is referring to the ability to balance the 'schedule' with flexible, adaptive, responsive, timing of events.

The ability to do things at the 'right time' is the ability to identify the critical path as separate from the planned or indicative path. What are the activities in the schedule that must occur on a specific day for the ultimate deadline to be achieved? What is the best time considering dependencies and environment to undertake other planned activities?

How it fails ...

Project scheduling is often managed by an individual who plugs in, tracks and revises all project activities to keep the implementation on track. This individual is skilled in the software and has an understanding of milestones, dependencies and managing a critical path, though is likely not adept at considering the 'best' timing for activities to occur in the context of stakeholders' responses to change. They are scheduling the outputs not the outcomes. Outcomes, that involve people's emotional responses, cannot be scheduled.

Why it fails ...

Accepting that there are aspects of a project schedule that are outside of your control is a challenging concept for project management. The key skill is to identify what is within your span of 'influence'. A flexible, adaptive, responsive approach to things that are 'outside of your control', but within your span of influence, needs to be established, so that the right activities can occur at the right time to ensure success.

In complex, expensive, high risk, challenging project environments it is often a big ask to add a layer of uncertainty to the schedule. It requires an expert degree of confidence to identify the degree of flexibility that is required to ensure the success of individual activities and the ultimate realisation of the project aims.

Agile thinking can alleviate some of these issues. However, it is dependent on the overall size, scope and complexity of the program.

RIGHT PEOPLE
Why it's important

Having the right people involved in project activities can make or break the success of a transition. Reputation and precedence for the selection of project participants plays out in change programs all the time. A project team is formed based on the most likely individuals who have demonstrated capability or experience previously. An executive sponsor is typically the most likely person, the business representatives and SMEs are the people who have been in these roles before. This selection on precedence is usually a good place to start. However, you should consider their cultural fit for where you are headed. I have witnessed transformations get off track because resources were the right fit to begin with but as the organisation changed around them – became the obstacle for the objectives to be realised.

Time and time again, executive teams reflect at the 3/4 point in a change program about the 'unlikely' people that come out of the woodwork and shine. These are people that haven't previously felt empowered or been in a position to be 'self-actualising'. These are the people that drive cultural change and will bring new, innovative ways of working to your organisation.

Identifying, including and supporting these individuals as they emerge will assist in the mix of having 'the right people' driving your change. All of these resourcing considerations require a degree of flexibility and the courage to make some difficult and courageous decisions along. It is perfectly okay to say 'you've done a fantastic job, and now we need to look at the next phase and resource mix that we require to achieve our objectives.'

How it fails ...

If the individuals forming and participating in the project are the same individuals who usually drive change in your organisation, it is likely that what changes and how it changes will be similar to previous initiatives. This may or may not be your aspiration for the change. Consider the behavioural and cultural changes that are desired to support the change being implemented and to communicate what these changes and aspirations look like so as to inspire and encourage the individuals who are like-minded to those aspirations to be empowered to step into leadership of the change. These people may surprise you, may seem to be almost like a 'different person' when they step into these positions to support the change.

Often, aspects of a program will fail with the wrong person at the helm. Organisations in transition usually need a turnover of change leadership as the cyclic nature of change often results in a loss of effectiveness around the 9-12 month point (due to burnout, lack of resilience, loss of objectivity). If an organisation or a program team are unwilling to be flexible in resourcing the change, the natural flow of the 'right people' becoming involved (doing the right things at the right time) may stagnate the change and benefits being fully realised (Too much in Awareness).

Why it fails ...

So often, people want to 'help' – and they do this by controlling and making decisions on behalf of other people. Usually these decisions are based on assumptions. Using the Jo-Hari window as a frame of reference we are reminded that there are many unknown unknowns (we don't know, what we don't know). Acknowledging and working in a space of unknowns can be unsettling in complex programs that require high degrees of control to ensure a project is delivered on time and on budget, but unearthing the unknowns about 'people' can often be the very thing that truly transforms an organisation. If there is an unwillingness to 'open the playing field' and to continually review and adjust the involvement of individuals in a program, opportunities to change will be lost (activities on Transferable skills can assist here).

RIGHT WAY
Why it's important ...

A project manager will generally focus on delivering tasks, outputs and activities to schedule 'the what'. A change manager will be focused mostly on 'the how'. There has been a trend to 'blend' project and change management into one role, however successful transformations need both, someone focused on the what and someone focused on the how, it is the tension between these two driving forces that delivers the best results.

Too much focus on the 'what' increases the risk that the changes won't be adopted. Too much focus on the 'how' increases the risk of not delivering to the schedule and budget. Undertaking the right things, at the right time, with the right people also requires delivery in the right way to ensure success.

The right way will be aligned to your values and your desired culture, inclusive, structured, organised, confidence building, professional, tested, grounded, considered, evidence based, facilitated, supportive and supported.

How it fails ...

When the drivers to get things done – amplified by short timeframes, competing priorities and complex environments – is greater than the need to do things well, consideration of 'the right way' often won't get a look in. It is at this point that change leaders need to use their change strategies to build and demonstrate why a continued focus on the right way is required. It is important to specify how the program will get off track if the program takes short cuts on engagement, inclusion, accountability and ownership. A change leaders influencing skills are critical at this point, and it is why experienced change leadership is required. If change leaders are not trusted advisors in positions of authority to provide this balanced view to guide the organisation through challenging periods of change it is unlikely that the anticipated benefits will be fully realised.

Why it fails ...

Change fails when the change resources have not been project resources and vice versa. Inexperienced leadership that is not adept and managing both the 'what' and the 'how' will cause an unconstructive friction. While a project manager could also be the change manager, and vice versa, if experienced in the other field, the two roles need an understanding of one another to ensure that healthy debate on approaches, resourcing, timelines and engagement can occur. All too often 'experts' in their field lack the ability to compromise and adjust their approaches to deliver the program in 'the right way'.

19

We've Got This

There is a point in every change program when you pass the tipping point and you can be confident that you are well on the way to achieving the destination.

The specialist resources you have supporting the change, whether they are internal or external, will likely see this before everyone else. They will be looking for this point in the program and will be aware that you are reaching this point even before the executive sponsor, steering committee, executive team and leadership at all levels.

It is a subtle shift of accountability. If the Change Approach has been a trusted support model, it is likely that throughout the program, the change team have been included in everything, seen as the people that resolve problems, know all the answers and always respond with a positive attitude.

The sign of a successful change program should leave the change team feeling redundant. If it is a particularly successful program where you have built internal change capabilities, networks and support mechanisms, this will likely occur before implementation. If your change program has built confidence and encouraged ownership where everyone knows what is changing, how it's changing, why it's changing and when it's changing and is ready to adapt, then the job of the change team has been done.

There is a point, however, where the rubber hits the road and internal resources will want to focus on what needs to be done to get this thing over the line. The focus at this stage of a project will be internal management practices, conversations on managing business risk, switching core operations from the old ways to the new ways. This will be most successful if led by direct line managers.

The organisation most likely won't see that this shift has occurred, yet change resources will be able to identify this shift as it is occurring and can be typified by:

- No longer being involved in discussions or meetings
- Materials being released without being first 'run through' the change team
- Content being 're-worked' as operational documents (ownership)
- Activities being re-branded from program initiatives to BAU initiatives

Often at this point, the organisation will still feel as though it needs the change support, even as they have stopped relying on the assistance. It is critical for external change resources to step back at this point and strike a new balance of supporting rather than leading.

The change team should draw back and stop creating documents; rather, they should be led and owned by internal resources. The change team's focus should be on the transfer of knowledge and the capability to uplift. Meetings and support forums should be facilitated by internal resources with external change resources on hand through the transition period.

There are some interesting behaviours that subconsciously crop up from key stakeholders at this point in the program. They are generally the result of individuals trying to 'take back control' once they are feeling comfortable in their role leading change. There are some unconstructive ways that individuals may do this: excluding individuals and their advice, undermining their authority, or their opinions and dismissing their work.

Whilst these are not behaviours that are conducive to healthy working relationships, it is worthwhile exploring the root cause. This is a nice demonstration of stakeholders who have been 'too-much' in the Guidance Element (i.e. someone else will make this happen). The poor behaviours surface when they are trying to take accountability. Responding to the poor behaviours and not their intention to take accountability will make the situation worse. All leaders in the organisation should constantly be on the lookout for evidence of stakeholders saying or showing 'we've got this' as this moment in the program is when stakeholders either take ownership and make the change stick or back away because they haven't been empowered to step in and take the lead.

20

Core Capabilities

There are a range of capabilities that are vital to for all change leaders. Many have been referred to throughout this book, however, there are three that stand out consistently as the core capabilities. Throughout this chapter, the three key takeaways for managing change have been explored in more detail and recommendations for building the skills are provided.

1. DON'T MAKE ASSUMPTIONS.
Why is it important?

Assumptions are the enemy of adoption. Adoption requires ambiguity and uncertainty so that ownership and accountability fill the void on unknown aspects of the change. Assumptions may form part of your day-to-day role in operational decision making, but they play no role in facilitating individuals through change. Assumptions in this context relate to what you could possibly never know about other individuals and their responses to change.

Why is it so hard?

As humans, we like to help, to know, to be in control. We even like progress. Often the information that we don't know can seem like it's preventing us from moving forward and so we fill the void…with assumptions. When dealing with people and their responses to change, it can be detrimental to someone's journey to make assumptions as it takes their power away and their ability to adopt to the change in their own way and in their own time.

Build the skill

- Jo-Hari window – build your awareness of people's knowns and unknowns.
- Call-out – agree in a peer group a friendly way to say, 'That sounds like an assumption.'
- Ladder of inference – explore to learn how very little you know of other people's influencers.
- Not about me – build your own awareness as to what responses are about you and what belong to someone else.

2. BUILD CONFIDENCE.
Why is it important?

With confidence literally being 'full of trust', you will need to build trust with stakeholders regarding their involvement. This includes, how they will be communicated with, the reliability of messages, that if they invest time and emotionally in the change that it will actually happen. Change programs invariably rely on cascading messages as a primary communication point, as research continually suggests that staff prefer to receive messages from their direct line managers. This communication and engagement point will fail if there is no trust that the change will deliver the anticipated benefits and that the change process will be managed smoothly.

Why is it so hard?

We all have our own experiences of previous change. Most individuals can identify a time in their personal or professional lives where a change has been disappointing, or that the process of change was hard. These previous experiences will influence an individual's ability to engage fully in a change until confidence has been built…and maintained. Never miss a deadline or fail to deliver against what has been communicated throughout the entire program. This becomes difficult to manage, as details are being worked through and there will be those periods of ambiguity and uncertainty. The core skill here is to identify what can and can't be communicated through these periods of time. It is critical to maintain the momentum by continuing to communicate through these periods or individuals will fill the void with rumours that will be damaging to confidence in the program.

Build the skill…

Brainstorm something you can say for everything you can't. Conceptually separate planned activities and likely scenarios, then tailor messages to cover both scenarios. Polish your materials – aim to provide any messages as though they were a professionally designed brochure. Productise your channels of communication – fact sheets, posters, forums, panels, symposiums. Remember: only communicate dates that you are 100% confident you will deliver against.

3. STEADY THE COURSE.
Why is it important?

Common phrases at the transition point of any implementation are 'Hold the line', 'Maintain the rage', or 'Steady the course'. When stakeholders arrive at the 'rubber hitting the road' point of a change, the temptation is to take ownership (which is perfect) and do things their own way (not so perfect, as it impacts confidence-building approach). There will be a lot of noise and there will be feedback from all directions, which will be specific to an individual's needs and not necessarily a required correction to the whole program. It is common for communication channels to start to lose their effectiveness, but it is critical to maintain them. If a change to the approach is required, consider it as a 'value-add', not a complete overhaul.

Why is it so hard?

As people start to engage more in a change that is becoming real to them, the instinct to 'help' will kick in. This instinct to help will most likely be influenced by individuals 'ladder of inference' but can often be delivered with so much vigour and passion, that it is difficult to say no. When leaders hear these impassioned pleas, their likely response will be 'also to help' and respond to requests to change the approach, agree there are gaps, appoint new resources, and communicate a timeline that they haven't worked through yet, whether or not they can meet it. There are, of course, circumstances where you genuinely may need to re-think and respond to what stakeholders are asking for, but a well-planned program with established channels should not find itself in this position.

Build the skill

Educate all stakeholders, early in a program, on likely responses to change. Include stakeholders in the early development of channels, so they feel ownership on what they look like. Continually, i.e. every time you deliver something, ask if it meets stakeholder needs (embedding this approach early, will minimise any backlash to the established approaches at the transition point). Continually re-iterate 'the steps that got us here' including all points of stakeholder involvement, this technique is like a rudder that helps to steer staff to the next engagement point.

USING YOUR CORE CHANGE CAPABILITIES

Focus in the last twenty years has been on 'productising' change assessment tools, monitoring and measuring how well the change is being adopted in an organisation. It is likely that whether or not you use these measurement tools, you will still be undertaking the same activities.

The Transformation[3] approach encourages the ongoing 'review/respond' life cycle of real time humanistic assessment. Primarily it is through conversations that you will know how the change is tracking. Moment in time checkpoints usually delivered through surveying stakeholders provide little additional value to talking with stakeholders, as you should be able to predict the results based on where you are in the program and through the range of engagement channels you have established. This 'no survey' approach is encouraged because if you talk to people you will hear one of two responses: 'We're okay'; 'We're not okay'.

If you then ask the right questions and listen to people, you will hear:

- We know where we are now, but we don't know where we're headed. (Too-much in Awareness)
- We know where we're headed, but it's such a long way from where we are now. (Too much in Destination)
- We've got someone looking at that for us. (Too much in Guidance)

Each of these responses is indicative of where your transformation is. Talking and listening to people isn't just a way to assess where they're at, it's the way to shift the balance and move the program forward – a 'two for one', if you like.

Assessment tools focus on trying to map where people are. In reality, there are as many different responses to change as there are people in the world, and they are shifting from moment to moment. There are many different assessment tools available; you may have had an experience where you've invested in an assessment tool that was redundant the moment the report landed on your desk. Why didn't you spend that time talking to people?

What's a sure-fire way to ensure stakeholders feel that a change is being 'done-to them'? Send them a survey.

21

Transformation³ for Personal Growth

Whilst this book has been developed for organisational transformation. The Transformation³ methodology as you may have already gleaned is equally applicable to personal growth and life transformation.

You may have found yourself applying the concepts to your own personal circumstances, whilst also considering how it applies in your professional context. The concepts of the three elements in balance (Awareness, Destination, Guidance) are a powerful tool for assessing where you may be stuck, overwhelmed, or feeling powerless in achieving personal goals. As always, the first step is being aware of and understanding why you are feeling the way you do. The Transformation³ approach provides a framework for you to quickly and easily undertake a 'life diagnostic'. Once you know which elements are out of balance it is a simple process of undertaking activities that align to the elements that need to be re-balanced.

Whilst the content to support Transformation[3] for personal growth would be another book entirely, with the knowledge imparted in this book you can start to apply the thinking to all aspects of your personal and organisational transformations. The following section provides a summary of the types of activities that align to the three elements in a personal context. You may come up with your own too. The trick here is that you are naturally more wedded to the outcomes when it is about 'self' and so it can be challenging to be objective through this process and to hold yourself to account.

It can be helpful to find a peer that can listen and provide independent unbiased guidance to help validate your assessment of balancing your own elements. It can be tempting to do more of the activities that we enjoy doing but you can easily find yourself feeling more stuck, more overwhelmed and more powerless!

AWARENESS ACTIVITIES

FOR PERSONAL TRANSFORMATION
- Life audit (what are all the components in your life)
- Your CV/resume
- Your bio/story
- People audit (who is in your life)
- Readiness to change (environmental scan, dependencies, capacity)

- Impact assessment (who will be affected by your transformation and how)
- Clearly identified your 'Truth for Change' (what's not working, what's holding you back)

DESTINATION ACTIVITIES

FOR PERSONAL TRANSFORMATION

- What are your goals/your desired destination?
- What does success look like?
- What will the benefits be and when will they be achieved?
- What are the values that will support where you want to be
- What skills you are looking to develop?
- Be specific on finances, health, relationships, social, career
- What are the milestones along the way?

GUIDANCE ACTIVITIES

FOR PERSONAL TRANSFORMATION

- Reading (who are your favourite authors)
- Practitioners (who has been recommended as a good guide, coach, educator, counsellor, healer)
- Coach (who can hold you to account, do you need a coach)
- Seminars (what topics do you find inspirational)
- Development programs (what courses, skills, training are available that would assist you in achieving your goals)

- Friends (who in your network is supportive of where you are headed, who do you admire and or/see as leader)

Similar to the organisational approach, completing each of these activities is an ongoing undertaking, not a once-off activity. As you are transforming your life, what you have captured can be different just a few months later, so again don't assume that an activity has already been done. If you are observing the symptoms of your elements being out of balance it is well worth re-visiting any of these activities, in alignment with what the model is suggesting you should draw your attention to.

Lastly, they are called activities because they require action for the change to occur. Usually just exploring the elements is enough to inspire action as your path forward becomes clearer through applying the Transformation[3] approach. Often why we fail to take action in our personal transformations is the beliefs, attachments, experiences, that we have had in our lives to date that hold us back. Trusting the process, understanding that it will take time, and enjoying the journey are all helpful frames to create a space to take the next step forward.

If, in any moment, you don't feel stuck, you don't feel overwhelmed, or don't feel powerless, you are in the 'sweet spot' of how things transform. Keep doing exactly what you're doing!

22

A New Way of Thinking

As I was writing this book, I participated in a number of seminars and forums to assist in planning the dissemination of all this information that I am so passionate about sharing. I had a number of personal light-bulb moments sitting in these forums where I was physically aware of how I was feeling and the physiological responses I was experiencing in response to the speakers. I was aware of the simplest, and possibly most profound applications of Transformation[3] in my journey as an individual and my personal transformation.

I was critically aware of how uncomfortable I was in being 'too much' in the Guidance Element, I like taking accountability, so sitting in a room being talked at for two days felt like I was losing time to be productive, have ownership, deliver value and simply do the work. I was also aware that I was feeling overwhelmed by being too much in the 'Destination

Element' all of the advice provided made me aware of the amount of work that I needed to do to reach my desired destination, work that takes three, five, ten years to achieve and I wanted to be there now.

I was able to, in those moments, 'balance the elements' and my ability to 'transform myself' my state of being, smoothly, in the room, in real time, by this simple process. One technique was by simply capturing these thoughts, then re-focusing on the 'Awareness' element: where I was at in that moment, and what was going on for me physically, emotionally, mentally.

As I followed these experiences, it dawned on me in how many ways the Transformation[3] elements play out in our personal transformations as well as our professional transformations. One example that is universally relatable is what we all experience when embarking on a career change and the dreaded resume updating process. In the early years of my corporate career, I spent some time at an executive search firm and in this role looked at thousands of executive resumes. Since then, I have found myself offering freely to review many resumes for friends, peers, and clients. I find it easy to identify the improvements required, and love to help people transform their lives. I am always aware of how people struggle with this process, and I too have resisted the ego-centric process of capturing personal achievement.

It occurred to me that in the context of Transformation[3] that when we write or update our resume, we are doing an 'Awareness' activity, but are doing so in the context of the 'Destination' element. We are trying to capture who we are and what we have done but are doing so whilst we are focusing on 'where we want to be'. This immediately causes an internal conflict of authenticity, finding it difficult to appropriately select and frame what we have done. What can be even more confronting is trying to define who we are in the context of 'what someone else needs'.

When confronted with this paradigm, individuals generally and naturally, gravitate to the 'Guidance Element' to help bridge the gap and naturally help them through their transition. They ask someone external for help, recruiters, coaches, peers, family. They look online at current research and how-to guides, they download templates, they talk to their referees. All these activities bridge the gap and assist in a better outcome.

The resume example is evident when you receive a poorly crafted resume that captures some things that an individual has done but isn't at all aligned to the role they have applied for! It is not, often as we assume, that this individual hasn't had the relevant experience or isn't the right person for the job – they've just been too stuck in one of the elements to write an appropriate reflection of themselves and what they have to offer.

There are so many examples of the elements in play in our daily lives we are constantly self-managing ourselves through change; when we buy a new car or move house, take holidays try a new diet and so on. Starting to use this model in your own life is a powerful way of embedding this new way of thinking. Once you embed the model in daily practice you will easily be able to ensure in your transforming organisation that individuals, groups, programs, functions all remain in the sweet spot and can sustain the level of organisational change that is now the new norm.

There are many instances however, where this natural 'balancing of the elements' does not occur, and you can probably now identify either at present or in the past, many examples of individuals or organisations showing symptoms that they are out of balance.

Epilogue

In the Preface of this book I highlighted my passion for the human experience which has likely been evident throughout the contents presented in this book.

I consider imparting these observations and learnings part of enabling and empowering the 'modern explorer'. I define the modern explorer as people that are passionate about growth and understanding and inspiring new ways of thinking, being and experiencing. The final statements I will share are a guiding set of reminders to help us navigate this new way of being.

Thank you for taking the time to consider the ideas presented in this book and in your own way, embarking on the journey of the modern explorer.

' We live in an age where information is all around us, we can find whatever we require, it is pervasive and overwhelming. For us to progress beyond the information age, we need to step beyond knowledge and seek wisdom.

' We need to challenge each other by being vulnerable to 'not knowing' and open to 'seeking'. We need to challenge the status quo and re-think at a new pace, using the web of information to guide us, but not to drive us.

' We need to be driven by our values, not by just defining who we want to be, but by living it and challenging our inner selves to overcome the hurdles and the obstacles that prevent us from achieving beyond our pre-conceived notions of success.

' We need to be comfortable being exposed in our own truths and support one another to ride the waves of learning and growth, we need to see our failures as successes and find new ways to rise over the peaks of the insurmountable as individuals and groups.

' We need to be brave in setting a Vision and charting a course by being humble in our 'Truth for Change'.

' We need to be present in each moment with ourselves and fellow voyagers and create and shape in every moment.

Tomorrow's blank page belongs to you ...